TOUGH QUESTIONS—BIBLICAL ANSWERS

TOUGH QUESTIONS—BIBLICAL ANSWERS

Jack Cottrell

College Press Publishing Company, Joplin, Missouri

2nd Printing 1986
3rd Printing 1988
4th Printing 1989

Printed and bound in the
United States of America

All quotations from Scripture are from the New American Standard Bible unless noted otherwise.

Library of Congress Catalog Card Number: 85-072669
International Standard Book Number: 0-89900-208-0

TABLE OF CONTENTS

PREFACE

This book is based on the conviction that the Bible is God's inerrant word given for all mankind, and that it presents the framework of a total life-and-world view. Its doctrine and its ethical principles are relevant to the social and moral issue of all times. Until we learn to use the Bible and apply it to such problems as capital punishment, genetic engineering, homosexualism, and labor strikes, we will be at the mercy of today's humanistic value-shapers and our own uninformed feelings.

This book is actually a sequel to an earlier volume entitled *The Bible Says* (Cincinnati: Standard Publishing, 1982). The two together are intended to cover the four major areas of ethical concerns. The first volume dealt with (1) problems relating to justice and human government and (2) issues of life, death, and personhood. This volume covers (3) issues relating to marriage and sexuality, and (4) problems of stewardship and economics.

Since the time when the first volume appeared, however, it has gone out of print. Because the original publisher opted not to reprint it, and declined to print this sequel at all, they are both now being issued by College Press, but under a different title—and in reverse order.

The reader may ask, "Why is the *sequel* now bing printed as *Volume I*?" The answer is that the order was reversed so that the book which had not yet been printed (i.e., this one) could be made available first. Thus, though this work was originally intended to follow the other one, it is now Volume I in the new format. The original *The Bible Says* will be published in a slightly revised form as Volume II of *Tough Questions — Biblical Answers* in 1986.

It is hoped that the material in both books will enable us to see the relevance of our familiar slogan, "The Bible alone is our only rule of faith *and practice.*"

Jack Cottrell
August, 1985

1

MARRIAGE

The most important human relationship is marriage—the relationship between husband and wife. It is more important than ties to home and parents (Gen 2:24), since the future literally depends upon the one-flesh union. It also takes priority over one's relation to his or her children. This does not mean that the latter is unimportant. It means rather that success in child-rearing depends very much upon the maintenance of a successful relationship between the mother and the father.

Since it is so important, we should want to know as much as possible about marriage. We must not assume that a person of marriageable age automatically or naturally knows everything he needs to know about it. Animals may know instinctively how to mate; but man is more than an animal, and marriage is more than sexual mating. We must be *specifically taught* about the nature of marriage, and our best teacher is the Word of God.

In this chapter we shall present what the Bible says about the essence of marriage. We shall also attempt to relate the Biblical teaching to a number of specific issues such as singleness, polygamy, and intermarriage with non-believers.

I. *Ordained By God*

The first thing to note about marriage is that it is a relationship ordained by God himself from the very creation of mankind. Adam and Eve were *created* as "husband and wife." God's first recorded instructions to them were to "be fruitful and multiply, and fill the earth" (Gen 1:28).

The second chapter of Genesis gives a detailed account of the creation first of the man, then of the woman. The woman was specifically made to be a companion and helper for the man (Gen 2:18). After the process of her creation is described, the divine commentary states, "For this cause a man shall leave his father and his mother, and shall cleave to his wife; and they shall become one flesh" (Gen 2:24).

Jesus refers to these very words as the ultimate ground of the marriage relationship (Matt 19:4, 5). Thus, he says, a husband and wife are in the final analysis joined together by God himself (Matt 19:6).

Because marriage is given by God, it is under His authority and control. Whenever the Bible speaks on a matter pertaining to marriage, that is the final word. It is not just a civil or legal issue, but a religious and moral one.

It is appropriate, however, for marriage to be regulated by civil authorities. Here we must remember the purpose of government, which in part is to protect the innocent from injustice and exploitation by the lawless and unscrupulous. Thus the state may make the responsibilities of marriage a *legal* requirement (in addition to a moral requirement), in order to protect a spouse from arbitrary abandonment or a child from neglect. The state may also specify who is authorized to sanction a marriage. Christians, of course, should abide by all such civil regulations as long as these do not require direct disobedience to a law of God.

Sometimes the civil laws regarding marriage (and divorce) do not conform to God's law. Civil regulations are often more lenient and allow certain things not permitted by Scripture, such as marriage between believers and non-believers, or divorce for practically any reason. In such cases we must remember that God's law prevails: the fact that something is *legal* does not mean it is *right*.

II. *A Union of Two Lives*

A second point about the essence of marriage is that it is a real union of two lives into one. The word *union* literally means *oneness;* to unify means to one-ify or to make one. When two people marry, they are joining their lives into one life. A man "cleaves" to his wife, and they become "one flesh" (Gen 2:24). They are "joined together" (Matt 19:6).

We must now note several things about this union.

A. *A Complementary Relationship*

First, the marriage union is a *complementary* relationship. When God had created Adam he observed, "It is not good for the man to be alone; I will make him a helper suitable for him" (Gen 2:18). Man and woman are designed to complement each other, that is, to *complete* each other. Together they form a whole life (they become "one flesh").

This shows that marriage is meant to be the norm or ideal state for man. This is contrary to the teaching of the Roman Catholic Church, which says that celibacy is the ideal and is "more spiritual" than marriage. It is also contrary to a growing tendency in contemporary Protestantism to glorify the single state and to present it as an option that is in itself equal or even superior to marriage. This is simply not so. It is *not good* for man to be alone. (See I Tim 4:3; Heb 13:4).

On the other hand, marriage is not morally necessary; nor is it *morally* superior to singleness. The married person is not "more spiritual" than his single counterpart. The Hebrew word for "good" in Genesis 2:18 can (and here does) mean "pleasant" or "beneficial," as in "Good morning!" It does *not* imply that singleness is less than *morally* good.

Indeed, there are many cases where a person is single through no fault of his own (Matt 19:12). By God's grace and the support of others he may learn to accept his situation and to cope with it. But we do no one a favor when we artificially exalt singleness as a generally desirable or even preferable state.

We must acknowledge that sometimes singleness may be desirable or preferred *in view of special circumstances.* In certain kinds of situations it *is* better to remain single. Jesus speaks of those who "made themselves eunuchs for the sake of the kingdom of heaven" (Matt 19:12). In other words, a person may sacrifice marriage if he is able to perform more effective service thereby, as Paul also advises in I Corinthians 7:32-34.

In chapter 7 of I Corinthians, however, Paul seems to be speaking of what is preferable, i.e., *expedient*, only in view of some imminent threat to the church. As he says in verse 26, "I think then that this is good in view of the present distress." He does not specify the nature of that distress; it may have been "the things about which you wrote" (verse 1). In any case Paul does say that in view of certain threatening circumstances, it may be preferable to remain single (verses 1, 8). Even in this situation, though, if a person cannot remain single without sinning, he should marry (verses 2-7).

The main point is that God created man and woman in such a way that their lives lack completeness until they are joined in marriage. Their lives are meant to be shared with one another by God's design.

B. *An Exclusive Relationship*

Second, the marriage union is an exclusive relationship. The intrusion of a third party necessarily destroys the wholeness or oneness formed by the joining of one man with one woman. Thus a wife's commitment to her husband excludes any kind of romantic or erotic attachment to any other man. Likewise, a man's commitment to his wife means that she alone will be the object of his desires. The modern concept of an "open marriage," where by mutual consent the marriage partners are free to seek liaisons elsewhere, does not even deserve to be called a marriage.

The exclusive nature of the husband-wife relationship also rules out polygamy (and polyandry) as an acceptable option. In the beginning God created *one* man and *one* woman, thereby forming the divine pattern for marriage forever. In answering a question about divorce, Jesus calls attention to this fact (Matt 19:4, 5). The two—not three or four or more—shall become one flesh. Why, then, did great men of the Old Testament, such as Abraham and Jacob and David, have more than one wife? The words of Jesus concerning the Mosaic law of divorce probably apply here: God permitted it because of the hardness of hearts, but from the beginning it was not so (Matt 19:8).

C. *A Total Union*

Third, the marriage union is a *total* union. It involves the uniting of two lives on every level, both physical and spiritual. Union on the physical level is certainly seen in the reference to "one flesh." Sexual intercourse as the union of two bodies is thus part of the very essence of marriage. They truly become as one body, since the body of each spouse becomes the common possession of both. "The wife does not have authority over her own body, but the husband does; and likewise also the husband does not have authority over his own body, but the wife does" (I Cor 7:4).

But marriage must be more than sexual union. Sexual intercourse is in itself such a powerful uniting force that even an act of prostitution results in "one flesh" on at least a physical level (I Cor 6:13-16). Does this mean that whenever two people engage in even casual sex, they are automatically married? No, because marriage requires *more* than a union of bodies. It requires union also on the spiritual level—a mutual commitments to share not only bodies but whole lives: beliefs, desires, hopes, fears, plans, joys, sorrows, feelings, weaknesses, and strengths. It requires, as we commonly say, a marriage *vow,* which is a mutual spiritual covenant.

This spiritual aspect of the marriage union is the reason why the Bible absolutely forbids a believer (a Christian) to marry a non-believer. This Biblical prohibition, though commonly ignored by God's people, is one of the most important aspects of God's law for marriage.

A basic principle of Scripture is the separation that must be maintained between God's own people and the people of the world. There is in reality a spiritual distance between believers and non-believers. Their spiritual orientations are totally different; they have nothing in common, nothing to share. Because of this actual incompatibility of lives and life-styles, and because of the danger of spiritual corruption, God has commanded his people to keep themselves separate from non-believers. This does not rule out *all* associations, especially redemptive ones; but it does prohibit any intimate relationships of mutual sharing and fellowship, of which marriage is the pre-eminent example.

From the time when God first chose a special people and set them apart from the world in general, he has required this separation. In Leviticus 20:24, 26 he told the people of Israel, "I am the Lord your

God, who has separated you from the peoples. . . . Thus you are to be holy to Me, for I the Lord am holy, and I have set you apart from the peoples to be Mine.'' He gave them specific instructions not to fellowship with their pagan neighbors, and especially not to intermarry with them. Here are the Lord's words from Deuteronomy 7:2-4:

> You shall make no covenant with them and show no favor to them. Furthermore, you shall not intermarry with them; you shall not give your daughters to their sons, nor shall you take their daughters for your sons. For they will turn your sons away from following Me to serve other gods. . . .

See also Exodus 34:12-16. The same warning appears in Joshua 23:12-13:

> For if you ever go back and cling to the rest of these nations, these which remain among you, and intermarry with them, so that you associate with them and they with you, know with certainty that the Lord your God will not continue to drive these nations out from before you; but they shall be a snare and a trap to you, and a whip on your sides and thorns in your eyes. . . .

When the Israelites failed to heed God's command against intermarriage, spiritual corruption followed and God's wrath came upon them. See Judges 3:5-8; I Kings 11:1-11. In the days of Ezra and Nehemiah they were forced to face up to this problem and to begin heeding God's law against these sinful unions. See Ezra 9:1—10:12; Nehemiah 13:23-27. Several times in these passages intermarriage is referred to as *unfaithfulness to God.*

The strongest statement of this Bible principle of separation is found in II Corinthians 6:14-18. The commandment is specific: "Do not be bound together with unbelievers'' (verse 14); "Come out from their midst and be separate'' (verse 17). Verse 14 literally says, do not be *unequally yoked* with unbelievers. The picture is that of a double yoke made for one kind of animal—such as oxen—in which two totally different kinds of animals have been joined together—such as an ox and a goat.

Why does God prohibit spiritual unions with non-believers? Because the parties in such a union are spiritually incompatible. This is stressed in the most emphatic way possible in a series of contrasts:

> What partnership have righteousness and lawlessness, or what fellowship has light with darkness? Or what harmony has Christ with Belial, or what has a believer in common with an unbeliever? Or what agreement has the temple of God with idols? For we are the temple of the living God (II Cor 6:14-16).

If this passage has any application at all, it certainly must apply to marriage. We cannot continue to close our eyes to the fact that God does not approve of a marriage between a believer and a nonbeliever. The Christian life is of such a nature that there is *no basis* for spiritual communion ("What has a believer in common with an unbeliever?") and the marriage relationship in its very essence *is* a spiritual union.

This means that a Christian should condition his thinking to the point that he would never even *consider* marrying a nonbeliever. Parents must take the initiative here and begin to instill this idea in the minds of their children very early, even before they start to think about dating. Ministers and youth leaders should also stress this point. (Whether a Christian can *date* a nonbeliever is a matter of opinion. Since dating is usually a prelude to marriage, however, it may be expedient to avoid even this kind of "unequal yoke.")

The fact that a believing spouse sometimes converts the unbelieving mate is no justification for intermarriage. One can never be sure this will happen, and the opposite *may* occur. We must not confuse marriage with evangelism. (If one partner in a marriage is converted and *becomes* a believer, and the other one does not, then I Corinthians 7:12-16 applies.)

Ministers can help to restore this aspect of holiness by refusing to perform marriages between believers and nonbelievers. In fact, I believe this is the only consistent position for a minister to take. If such intermarriage is wrong, then it is wrong to perform the ceremony. The fact that "someone else will do it if I don't" is no reason for going against God's law. A Christian doctor could use the same rationalization for performing abortions: "If I don't do it, someone else will." Such is hardly sound ethical reasoning!

Ministers who decide to take this stand should be prepared for all sorts of ill will and accusations from those who will not accept it. It is best to state one's convictions on this matter clearly and early. Elders should formulate such a policy for their congregations.

The most problematic aspect of this issue is the definition of a "believer" in today's fragmented and diluted Christendom. Some would define a believer as anyone who has membership in a "Christian" denomination. This is an easy solution, but I find it unacceptable. Are we willing to include a Catholic? or a cultist? or a nominal member only, with no real commitment? or a member of a liberal church that does not really believe in the Biblical Jesus? The safest way to be faithful to God's will regarding marriage is to define a believer as anyone who could be accepted, *as is*, as a member of your own local congregation.

Let us not lose sight of the main point. The marriage union is a *total* union, involving oneness on the spiritual level as well as the physical. Every spouse must work to cultivate both aspects.

III. *Covenant Love*

A final point is that marriage is a relationship of covenant love. Here is where the essence of marriage is most firmly grounded in God's own nature. God's relation to His people is often described in terms of marriage, where God is the husband and His people the wife (just as Christ is the bridegroom and the church His bride: Eph 5:22-23; II Cor 11:2; Rev 19:7; 21:2, 9).

The very essence of this relation between God and His people is covenant faithfulness and covenant love. Even when Israel committed spiritual adultery by following idols, like a faithful husband God remained true to His covenant vows (Jer 31:32). His love for His bride was so great that He was willing to forgive her most wanton behavior; His love was willing to say, "Nevertheless!" See Ezekiel 16, especially verses 53 and 60. See also Hosea 2:14-23. Ephesians 5:25-33 presents Christ's great self-sacrificing love for His church as the pattern for the loving relation between husband and wife.

This is the way we must view marriage. It is a covenant, a mutual commitment. It is a solemn promise in which each spouse vows to stand by the other and to love the other and to be faithful to the other forever. Young brides and bridegrooms should not think of marriage as an experiment or a trial, or as a tentative and conditional bond that is no stronger than a "granny knot" or a slip knot, ready to dissolve under the slightest pressure. Marriage is a permanent and exclusive commitment, and should never be thought of in any other way.

But is it possible for it to become and remain such in actuality, despite the contemporary pressures against it? Definitely, as long as the covenant is made and maintained in *love*. We are speaking not just of *eros,* or romantic love. We are speaking of *agape,* the caring and self-giving love with which God loves His bride; the love that loves "in spite of" and not "because"; the love that seeks not one's own happiness but the happiness of the other; the love that says, "Not my will, but *yours* be done." This is what makes a marriage "work," because this is what marriage is all about.

2

THE MEANING OF SEX

This chapter is not about the psychology of sex, nor the physiology and techniques of sex. It deals with something much more basic than these, namely, the theology of sex. We are concerned here with the meaning and intended purpose of sex among human beings as God created us. This will be the basis for our understanding of the morality of sex, to be discussed in the next chapter.

I. *Unacceptable Extremes*

How shall we understand our existence as sexual beings? A number of answers to this question have been suggested in addition to the Biblical one. Here we will briefly explain the two most common of these. One extreme puts sex in the animal category and says that any and all sex is always good; the other extreme puts it into the devil category and says that all sex is always bad. These views stand at opposite ends of the spectrum and are both unacceptable.

A. *The Animal View*

One of the most common views of sex today is that it is merely a natural animal appetite that can be gratified however one chooses, as long as he does not harm someone else. (This is the only qualification put upon it.) This is consistent with the modern naturalistic world view, which rejects the existence of God or at least His involvement in the affairs of men. Evolution and man's animal ancestry are presupposed, and human behavior is seen as just another form of animal behavior. This is how sex is understood.

An example of this view is the book *The Naked Ape* by the zoologist Desmond Morris (Dell, 1967). Morris begins his book with these words:

> There are one hundred and ninety-three living species of monkeys and apes. One hundred and ninety-two of them are covered with hair. The exception is the naked ape self-named *Homo sapiens.*

He continues, "The naked ape is an animal." Though it may be more intelligent than other species, "*Homo sapiens* has remained a naked ape nevertheless" (page 9).

How shall we understand man's sexuality, according to Morris? In the same way that we understand *all* human behavior, namely, by studying three sources: (1) the behavior of our evolutionary ancestors, as in fossil records; (2) the behavior of other living animals, "especially our closest living relatives, the monkeys and apes"; and (3) human behavior itself (pages 11, 12). The Bible is not mentioned.

In his long chapter on sex, Morris lets us know immediately that man's animal origin is the key to this aspect of his behavior: "To start with, he owes all his basic sexual qualities to his fruit-picking, forest-ape ancestors" (page 50). Any human peculiarities in this area are explained as quirks of evolution.

In a view such as this there is no basis whatever for moral restraints in any area, including sex. Sex is just an accident of nature, as is man himself. Since man himself is nothing special, sex has no special meaning or unique dimension among human beings.

Though not many have stated this view as cleverly and deliberately as Desmond Morris, it is nevertheless presupposed by a large portion of today's secularized society. Wherever evolution is accepted and God is rejected, this view will ultimately prevail. It explains the so-called "sexual revolution" of our time. Its logical corollary is "Anything goes."

A popular expression of the animal view of sex is the "Playboy Philosophy" of Hugh Hefner and others. This philosophy says that sex is just another physical appetite like thirst, and sexual activity is as ethically neutral as drinking a glass of water. It is a form of recreation, and casual sex with a friend or acquaintance is as innocent as a game of tennis.

B. *The Devil View*

At the other end of the spectrum is the view that sex is somehow an invention of the devil, and that all sexual activity, even within marriage, is evil (or nasty, or dirty). This view has been held by some pagans, especially dualistic groups like the Gnostics, who were contemporary with early Christianity. The Gnostics believed that matter as such, including our bodies, was created by an evil deity (called the "Demiurge") and is itself evil. Marriage and sex are the products of this same evil deity. As one group put it, the Demiurge created woman, and also created man from the navel downward. (This and much of the following information is found in chapter 3 of Derrick Bailey's book, *Sexual Relation in Christian Thought;* Harper, 1959.)

Unfortunately, something similar to this view found its way into Christendom quite early. Augustine (died A.D. 430) typified this thinking, and his influence swayed Christian thought for over a thousand years. Augustine taught that there was no sex prior to the first sin. If there had been, it would have been completely without passion and excitement, an act of will like planting seeds in a garden.

Now that sin has entered, said Augustine, sex is unavoidably accompanied by sinful desire and passion. All such desire is sinful lust, *even in marriage.* Even sex for procreation involves this lust, so that "even parents blush to think of what they have done together" (Bailey, page 55). Thus sex is always tainted by sin; it is "an unfortunate necessity to which the Christian should descend with regret" (Bailey, page 45).

This view prevailed through the early sixteenth century. At least in the beginning of his career Martin Luther himself looked at sex as a "regrettable yet imperative necessity" (Bailey, page 171).

Many Christians of all varieties continue to regard sex as something shameful, even between husband and wife. Many believe that sexual intercourse was *the sin* of Adam and Eve. In popular mythology sex is called "the forbidden fruit"; it is symbolized as an unclad woman licking her lips over an apple, with a snake looking on so that no one will miss the point. Similarly, it is still sometimes taught that the dimension of love called *eros* (sexual love) is evil.

Some call this the "Puritanical view," as if the Puritans were its prime representatives. This is an error, though. The Puritans were very strict in condemning sex outside of marriage, but they had a quite positive view of married sex.

The worst error, though, is to assume that this is the *Biblical* view of sex, and that nice people and good Christians should not enjoy sex even as husbands and wives. This results in a great deal of unnecessary guilt for many sincere believers, and it robs many marriages of one of their most important and delightful elements. This false assumption also brings reproach and ridicule upon Christianity from its enemies, as it gets the reputation of being life-negating, joy-denying, and pleasure-killing.

II. *The Biblical View of Sex*

The truth is that *neither* of the above extremes is the Biblical view. Unlike those who equate sex with sin, the Bible teaches that sex—including its passion and pleasure—is natural and good and has an important place in marriage. (The rest of this chapter will discuss this point.) But unlike the animal view, the Bible teaches that sex is natural but not morally neutral: within marriage it is good, but *outside* of marriage it becomes morally evil. (This will be discussed in the next chapter.)

It is most important to see that sex—man and woman as sexual beings—was created by God and is good when confined to the purpose for which it was designed. Genesis 1 shows that the origin of sex had nothing to do with sin. God created mankind as male and female and instructed them to be fruitful and multiply. This was a part of the situation He pronounced "very good" (Gen 1:27-31). Whether Adam and Eve actually made love prior to the first sin is irrelevant. God surely intended them to do so.

The additional details of the creation of Eve in Genesis 2 show the same thing. The woman was made from Adam and for Adam, so that they could become "one flesh." This chapter ends with a simple statement affirming the essential goodness of their sexuality: "And the man and his wife were both naked and were not ashamed" (Gen 2:18-25).

The entrance of sin did not alter the original purpose for sex. Adam's and Eve's acquired self-consciousness about their nakedness seems to be more related to their appearance before God than before each other. The nakedness of their bodies reminded them of the nakedness of their sinful souls before their righteous Maker. (See Heb 4:13.) Their attempts to hide their nakedness *from God* (Gen 3:7-11) were expressions of their fear and guilt from having disobeyed the commandment not to eat of the tree of knowledge of good and evil.

That sex remains essentially good even in the fallen world is clearly seen in a much-misunderstood Old Testament book, the Song of Solomon. Many Christians, laboring under the Augustinian error, have assumed that this Hebrew poem cannot be taken literally, because then it would have to be understood as actually talking about sex! Thus they have transformed the poem into a prophetic allegory depicting the spiritual love that Christ has for His church.

The fact is that this inspired book *is* about sex. It depicts, as one writer has said, "the intimate feelings and accents of married love." Even if it is intended to represent Christ's spiritual love for His bride, it still presents a positive view of the physical love between husband and wife.

The Song of Solomon, written mostly as a dialogue between bride and bridegroom, is not simply a blushing, grudging approval of marital sex. It is a virtual celebration of the delights of sexual passion and pleasure; it shows that a husband and wife can lovingly enjoy each other's bodies with the blessing of God. Consider these selections:

> The Song of Songs, which is Solomon's (1:1).
>
> May he kiss me with the kisses of his mouth!
> For your love is better than wine (1:2, bride speaking).
>
> How beautiful you are, my darling,
> How beautiful you are!
> Your eyes are like doves (1:15, bridegroom).
>
> How handsome you are, my beloved.
> And so pleasant!
> Indeed, our couch is luxuriant! (1:16, bride).

Like an apple tree among the trees of the forest,
So is my beloved among the young men.
In his shade I took great delight and sat down,
And his fruit was sweet to my taste (2:3, bride).

Let his left hand be under my head
And his right hand embrace me (2:6, bride).

O my dove, in the clefts of the rock,
In the secret place of the steep pathway,
Let me see your form,
Let me hear your voice;
For your voice is sweet,
And your form is lovely (2:14, bridegroom).

Your lips are like a scarlet thread,
And your mouth is lovely. . . .
Your neck is like the tower of David
Built with rows of stones. . . .
Your two breasts are like two fawns,
Twins of a gazelle,
Which feed among the lilies.
Until the cool of the day
When the shadows flee away,
I will go my way to the mountain of myrrh
And to the hill of frankincense. . . .
Your lips, my bride, drip honey;
Honey and milk are under your tongue,
And the fragrance of your garments is like the fragrance of
Lebanon (4:3-6, 11, bridegroom).

Awake, O north wind,
And come, wind of the south;
Make my garden breathe out fragrance,
Let its spices be wafted abroad.
May my beloved come into his garden
And eat its choice fruits! (4:16, bride).

The godly enjoyment of *eros* has been recently discussed at length in two books by Christian authors. One is *The Act of Marriage* by Tim and Beverly LaHaye (Zondervan, 1976); the other is *Intended for Pleasure* by Ed and Gaye Wheat (Revell, 1977). Two quotations from these authors sum up the point of this section: "God is the creator of sex. He set human drives in motion, not to torture men and women, but to bring them enjoyment and fulfillment" (LaHaye, page 14). "You have God's permission to enjoy sex within your marriage. He invented sex; He thought it up to begin with" (Wheat, page 16).

What has been said in this section must be qualified in two ways. First, it applies only to loving sex within marriage. This is clearly taught throughout the Bible. Hebrews 13:4 says it clearly: "Let marriage be held in honor among all, and let the marriage bed be undefiled; for fornicators and adulterers God will judge." Proverbs 5:15-20 offers this inspired wisdom:

> Drink water from your own cistern, and fresh water from your own well. . . . Let your fountain be blessed, and rejoice in the wife of your youth. As a loving hind and a graceful doe, let her breasts satisfy you at all times; be exhilarated always with her love. For why should you, my son, be exhilarated with an adulteress, and embrace the bosom of a foreigner?

Second, sex must be subordinated to the larger purposes of marriage, which it is intended to serve. In other words, sexual pleasure is not an end in itself, but is a means to other ends.

III. *Sex and Marriage*

Sex was made for marriage, not vice versa. But why? What purposes does sex serve in marriage? There are two: procreational and relational. The former is clear in Genesis 1:28, "Be fruitful and multiply." This is one reason why God has confined sex to marriage. Sex gets children, and children need to be reared in a family environment where there is a proper division of labor and proper role modeling.

In addition to procreation, and perhaps even more important, is the relational purpose of sex. Here we must recall the nature of marriage as a union of two lives on every level into a single shared life: "It is not good for the man to be alone" (Gen 2:18). Here we come to the most profound meaning of sex: it is designed to contribute to and reinforce this total oneness of husband and wife.

There is no question that sex has a tremendous uniting effect, as Paul indicates in his comments on union even with a harlot (I Cor 6:16). This is another reason—perhaps the main one—why God has confined sex to marriage. It was designed to bind two people together physically, emotionally, psychologically, and spiritually. It is totally inappropriate and even destructive outside marriage, where the participants have no intention of joining themselves together in a total union. It is like applying glue to two objects you do not really want to be stuck together. Once the glue has been applied, it is very difficult to get the objects unstuck without damaging one or both of them.

Sex has this effect because it is not just a physical act. The act itself involves more than the body; it involves the whole person. As a Christian counselor points out, "Even in the sex act itself we are reminded that this is a relationship of persons, not just bodies, for it is no coincidence that man is the *only* creature . . . who relates sexually face-to-face" (Wheat, pages 18, 19). But also, sex is more than just a single act. Husband and wife are sexual beings, and their marriage as a whole is a sexual relationship. It is punctuated throughout with such gestures as a wink, a pat, a touch, a kiss, a whisper—all of which have subtle sexual overtones, but are also tender expressions of love, approval, and oneness.

Here we can see the appropriateness of the term *know* as a common Biblical word for sexual union. (See Gen 4:1; Luke 1:34, e.g., in older translations.) Nothing opens up the total life of one person to another more than sex, or exposes one's whole self to another in a more intimate way. As LaHaye expresses it,

> . . . What better way is there to describe the sublime, intimate interlocking of mind, heart, emotions, and body in a passionately eruptive climax that engulfs the participants in a wave of innocent relaxation that thoroughly expresses their love? The experience is a mutual "knowledge" of each other that is sacred, personal, and intimate. . . . (page 15).

The powerful and satisfying pleasure achieved in sex is a key to its uniting effect. (Even secular writers have observed this and have coined the term "pleasure bond.") This is true in the sense that the pleasure one receives in sex tends to bond him to the one who gives that pleasure. But this is not the main point. Indeed, this in itself would be a rather selfish view. That is why the principal bonding effect of sex is not in the pleasure one *receives*, but in the pleasure one is able to *give* to his spouse. This is where *eros* becomes subject to *agape,* the very essence of which is the caring concern for the happiness of another. The general principle is stated in Philippians 2:4, "Do not merely look out for your own personal interests, but also for the interests of others.'' In the sexual relationship this means that one's greatest desire should be to give pleasure to the spouse. This is a natural expression of agape. Nothing can seal the marriage bond more securely than this mutual desire of the husband and wife to bestow on each other the gift of pleasure in their sexual relationship.

This, then, is the Biblical meaning of sex as it relates to marriage. Only on this background can we understand the morality of sex, to be discussed next.

3

THE MORALITY OF SEX

Whatever has great potential for good usually has great potential for evil if misused. Common examples are television and atomic power. This is also true of sex. Rightly used it is one of the most positive forces in God's creation, as seen in the last chapter. But if it is used contrary to God's design, it becomes a means of disruption and destruction in individual lives and in society too.

This is why God has placed such specific and firm boundaries around sex, in the form of Biblical commandments. In a way, a lot of "thou shalt nots" should be unnecessary. The positive teaching about the relation between sex and marriage should be sufficient to rule out extra-marital sex adventures. But so there will be absolutely no misunderstanding, God's law has spelled out for us the right *and wrong* uses of sex.

Of course it is not popular today to think in terms of sins and laws and absolute rights and wrongs, especially in relation to sex. But this is the way it is! Whether some people like it or not, we exist within the framework of God's moral law, and our sexual relationships are subject to this law.

Our response to God's commands regarding sex is an indication of just how serious we are about our total relationship to God. The level of sexual morality is usually a good barometer of general godliness or ungodliness, both for individuals and for societies as a whole. The further a person or society drifts from God, the more gross its sexual degeneration becomes. Unbridled and perverted sex is in effect a deliberate expression of defiance and rebellion against God. Paul shows in Romans 1:21-27 that once the restraints of belief in God and His authority are shed, licentiousness inevitably follows.

On the other hand, those who are close to God, who want to love and serve Him with all their hearts and minds and strength, will desire to know and to do God's will with regard to sex as with all else. This chapter is an attempt to summarize this one aspect of God's will.

I. *Immoral Deeds*

A. *The Big Two*

Sexual sin occurs on two levels: external and internal, deeds and thoughts. The "big two" among immoral deeds are pre-marital sex and extra-marital sex, or fornication and adultery. Despite the lax attitude toward these practices today, they always have been and always will be *sins*.

The New Testament word for fornication is actually a more general term and is often used to refer to any sexual activity outside of wedlock, whether by married or unmarried persons. Sometimes it is translated simply as "immorality" or "unchastity." (See II Cor 12:21; Gal 5:19; Eph 5:3; I Thess 4:3.) It can also be used for specific sins such as incest (I Cor 5:1), prostitution (I Cor 6:13, 18), and adultery (Matt 19:9).

What should be stressed, though, is that it can and does refer to pre-marital sex as such, which indicates that this *is* a sin in the sight of God. This point is sometimes challenged, usually in order to justify an immoral life-style. But the challenge fails: the Biblical term definitely includes old-fashioned fornication and condemns it as sinful.

Sometimes, for instance, the words *fornication* and *adultery* are used together in order to make it clear that fornication is something distinct from adultery, namely, *pre*-marital intercourse. *Both* violate the marriage bed, according to Hebrews 13:4. (See also Matt 15:19; I Cor 6:9.)

In I Corinthians 7 Paul clearly uses *fornication* in the sense of pre-marital sex. Under some circumstances, he says, it is better to stay single (verse 26); but if a person cannot control his sex drive, it is better to marry (verse 9). Verse 2 is very clear: in order to avoid *fornication,* let them marry. The New American Standard Bible has *immoralities* here, but the Greek word is usually translated *fornication.* Pre-marital sex is not an option, since it violates the very purpose of sex, which is to strengthen the marriage bond.

There is no question that the Bible condemns adultery, or sex by a married person with anyone besides his or her spouse. See Exodus 20:14 (the seventh Commandment); Leviticus 20:10 (where the death penalty is prescribed); Proverbs 6:20—7:27; I Corinthians 6:9; Hebrews 13:4. Adultery is treated as a heinous sin because it is a violation of the marriage covenant. As such it is an attack on the basic human institution, the family, and thus on the whole social order. (See Rousas Rushdoony, *Institutes of Biblical Law;* Craig Press, 1973; pp. 395-396.)

B. *Masturbation*

At this point we may comment on the difficult moral problem of masturbation. Many would condemn it outright, though often for the wrong reasons. In earlier times moralists sought to discourage this practice by blaming it for all sorts of maladies, including acne, impotence, insanity, weak eyes, and unusual growths of hair. There is no basis for such claims as these. Also, many have tried to find a reference to masturbation in the story of Onan in Genesis 38:4-10 (thus the term *onanism*), but there is really no parallel. In fact, there does not seem to be *any* specific reference to this practice in the Bible.

In recent times the trend has been to treat masturbation as a harmless outlet or "safety valve" for sexual tension. For instance, Lewis Smedes in *Sex for Christians* (Eerdmans, 1976) says it is nothing to worry about as long as it does not become compulsive or permanent (pages 160-164). Others treat it as a gift of God. Charlie Shedd in *The Stork Is Dead* (Word: 1968) with certain qualifications says, "Thank God for it and use it as a blessing!" (page 73).

While recognizing that there is no direct Biblical statement on the subject, I must conclude that masturbation is inconsistent with God's will in at least two ways. First, sex is for marriage and is designed to unite one person to another. Masturbation by definition is a solitary act. Second is the fact that lust is wrong, and it is very difficult if not impossible to separate masturbation from lust (in the form of sexual fantasies). This leads us to the next point.

II. *Immoral Thoughts*

The New Testament emphasizes the fact that sin does not have to involve an outward, visible act. Sin can occur in one's thought-life, completely unknown to any other person—except God. For instance, most people would never in their lives even think about actually murdering someone, but many of these same people harbor some kind of hatred in their hearts. In God's sight, hatred is a sin comparable to murder (I John 3:15).

A. *Entertaining Immoral Thoughts*

Sexual sin is like this. It can be overt and physical, as in the case of fornication or adultery. But it can also be something confined to the secret recesses of our minds, hidden from everyone but ourselves and our God. Jesus says it this way: "Everyone who looks on a woman to lust for her has committed adultery with her already in his heart" (Matt 5:28). This is mental adultery; and even though it may not have as many immediate consequences as physical adultery, it is a sin.

In his statement Jesus mentions only men and only adultery, but the principle obviously has a much broader application. Women are not immune from lusting after men, and such is equally sinful. Also, mental sexual sin is not limited to adultery. There can be mental fornication, incest, or homosexualism. Whatever is a sin in the overt act is also a sin though committed in the heart alone.

What is the nature of this sin? Sometimes we sum it up in one word: *lust.* It we want to be precise in our use of this word, we should notice that it basically means simply "a strong desire." On rare occasions the Greek term is used with a good connotation and is translated "desire" instead of "lust" (e.g., I Thess 2:17). Most often, though, it refers to evil lusts (Col 3:5), or the strong desire to do something evil.

Though such evil desires need not be limited to sexual matters, it seems that this is usually what is meant in the Biblical use of the term. This is of course the way Jesus used it in Matthew 5:28. (See Rom 1:24; I Thess 4:5; II Tim 3:6; I Peter 4:3. See also the more general references which probably include sexual lust, e.g., Rom 6:12; 13:14; Gal 5:24; II Tim 2:22; I John 2:16.) In some of these passages the New American Standard Bible reads "impulses" or "desires" instead of "lusts," but the Greek has various forms of the same word in all of them.

What actually constitutes lust? Does it include the mere observation (or admiration) of bikini-clad bodies on a beach? Does it include just *looking* at provocative pictures? Does it include enjoying a conversation with someone you think of as "sexy"? Does it include just thinking about the *possibility* of having an affair with an attractive neighbor?

It is probably not possible to exclude *all* sex-related sights and thoughts, but not all are necessarily equivalent to lust. Temptations are unavoidable; but being tempted is not the same as yielding to the temptation, nor is it the same as *wanting* to yield. The latter, it seems, is really what lust is. It is the actual *desire* for an immoral liaison with that person in the bikini, or in the picture, or in the tight slacks, or in the church choir. It is dwelling on and relishing the mental picture of a sexual relationship with that person. It is actually wanting or coveting such a relationship as is forbidden in the tenth Commandment, "You shall not covet your neighbor's . . . wife" (Exod 20:17).

We may not be able to avoid the temptations, but we *can* avoid this desire to yield to them. Of course we have the inner strength of the Holy Spirit to help us in this warfare (Rom 8:13; Eph 3:16), but the conquest of lust depends on our willingness to cooperate. What can we do? Jesus gives us the necessary plan of action immediately after His comment on adultery in the heart:

> And if your right eye makes you stumble, tear it out, and throw it from you. . . . And if your right hand makes you stumble, cut it off, and throw it from you; for it is better for you that one of the parts of your body perish, than for your whole body to go into hell (Matt 5:29, 30).

In other words, you know what incites lust in your own heart. Whatever it is, *avoid it! Get rid of it!*

If looking at bodies in bikinis incites you to lust, don't go to the beach! Don't listen to that music! Don't buy those magazines! If your problem is with a particular individual, cease all contact with that person (even if it hurts, like cutting off your hand). We have an obligation to separate ourselves from every cause of the sin of lust, and we *must* do so if we really want to conquer this sin.

B. *Inciting Immoral Thoughts*

One thing that makes lust so difficult to overcome is the fact that so many elements of our culture are actually *meant* to incite lustful feelings. Modesty is out; sexiness is in. Nudity is glorified; bare skin and skin-tight clothing are everywhere. What can we do about this?

Where we have no control over the actions of others, the only thing we can do is to avoid the source of incitement, as discussed above.

But we can do something more. We ourselves can avoid being a *cause* of lust in someone else by making sure our own dress and behavior are modest. If it is wrong to lust, then it is also wrong to cause someone to lust through immodest actions. No sincere Christian wants to be a stumbling block to a weaker brother or sister. If we simply follow the Biblical teaching here, there should be no problem.

The Bible enjoins modesty upon us in explicit terms (I Tim 2:9; see I Peter 3:1-4; Prov 11:22). Standards of modesty may differ from culture to culture, but one thing is sure: modesty is *not* determined by the fashion industry, but by what tends to incite lust in the beholder. Going without a bra may be fashionable, but if it causes others to stumble, it is wrong. Skin-tight jeans may be mod; but if they lead to leering, they are wrong. String bikinis may be in; but if they cause lust, they are out for the Christian.

The sad truth is that the very purpose of many fashions seems to be to stir sexual excitement in others (i.e., they are "sexy"). It is time for Christians to reject these ways of the world and to begin a modesty revolution. We can be neat and attractive without being indecent.

III. *The Lewd Mentality*

In addition to specific acts of sexual immorality and specific sins of lust, the Bible refers to a kind of person whose whole mentality and life-style are saturated with sexual sin. This is the person who is guilty of *sensuality* (lasciviousness, lewdness) and *impurity* (uncleanness). These Biblical terms refer to someone whose mind is continually "in the gutter," whose speech is vulgar, and whose life-style is promiscuous. They speak of the dirty-minded and the lewd, those who revel in smutty jokes, those whose principal goal is seduction, and those who plaster *Playboy* centerfolds all over their walls.

The Bible often includes one or both of these two terms (sensuality and impurity) in a cluster of terms referring to sexual immorality and a generally degenerate life-style. (See Rom 13:13; II Cor 12:21; Gal 5:19; Eph 5:5; I Peter 4:3.) The picture is sordid indeed, and is generally presented as the way of life from which the Christian has been rescued. In no way can a continuation of that sort of mentality be condoned in a believer.

A symptom of sensuality is filthy talk and dirty jokes (either listening to or telling them). Ephesians 5:4 specifically forbids this: "There must be no filthiness and silly talk, or coarse jesting, which are not fitting." Colossians 3:8 gives the command to put aside "abusive speech from your mouth." There is absolutely no excuse for a Christian to retain this vestige of paganism.

IV. *What About Contraceptives?*

One final question relating to sexual morality must be discussed, namely, birth control. Is it wrong for a husband and wife to use contraceptives? Some Christians think so. The Roman Catholic Church has consistently condemned every form of interference with the natural procreational purpose of sex. What is our answer? Yes and no. Contraception *in itself* is not wrong; but certain *forms* of birth control may be wrong, for reasons explained below.

Since the Bible says nothing specifically about this subject, we must base our conclusions on its general teachings about the purpose of sex in marriage. It is true that one purpose is procreation, but that is not its *only* purpose, nor even its *main* purpose. It may be wrong to want to exclude procreation altogether from one's marriage relationship, but it is not necessary to include it as a factor in every sexual encounter between husband and wife. Hence the wise use of contraceptives is right.

An important point that must be considered, however, is how the different methods of birth control work. This is an *extremely crucial* point: some contraceptives actually prevent conception, which is proper; but some work by *preventing a fertilized ovum from being implanted in the wall of the womb, which is equivalent to abortion.*

Which birth control methods actually cause such abortions? (1) The IUD, or intrauterine device. Its constant presence in the womb causes a mild chronic inflammation, thus usually preventing implantation. (2) The "morning-after" pill. It contains a drug that conditions the lining of the womb so that it rejects the just-begun baby. (3) *The* pill—sometimes. Since the time it was first introduced, the chemical makeup of the pill has been changed to reduce the chances of its causing a health problem in the user. But at the same time the change has made it likely that in some cases fertilization takes place but implantation does not (i.e., abortion). The frequency of this effect is not known; but generally speaking, the greater the progesterone (progestin) content of the pill, the greater the chance of its producing an abortion.

The pill's threat to the user's health is a separate consideration that may in itself raise moral questions about its use.

These are facts that every married couple should be aware of in the choice of a birth-control method. Those who oppose abortion and respect human life—even that which is newly conceived—will avoid the methods described above.

In conclusion, two words need to be stressed in relation to sexual morality. The first is *freedom*. Many complain that the Bible's restrictions on sex violate their freedom in this area. But the opposite is actually the case. As John White says in *Eros Defiled* (IVP, 1977), true freedom exists when persons or things are doing what they were designed to do. Sex was designed for marriage; thus true sexual freedom exists only when it is limited to this relationship (pages 51, 79).

The second word is *forgiveness*. Sexual sins, like any other sins, are forgiven through the blood of Christ to the repentant, faithful Christian. If God is willing to forgive these sins, we should be able to forgive one another—and to forgive ourselves. And if we truly love our gracious and forgiving God, we will do our utmost to maintain sexual purity.

4

HOMOSEXUALISM

The term *homosexualism* refers to sexual contact between persons of the same sex—male with male, female with female. Not everyone who engages in such acts is actually a homosexual. Some are experimenting; others are seeking perverse pleasures. A homosexual is one who truly is romantically attracted to others of the same sex.

It is estimated that about four percent of the population have an exclusively homosexual orientation, and that a total of about ten percent of the population have had considerable homosexual experience. Homosexual life-styles differ widely, ranging from unbridled promiscuity to pairs living together on a relatively permanent basis.

Thirty years ago a separate chapter on this subject would not have been necessary. There was a general consensus that homosexual activity is sinful. But the situation has changed considerably. In many circles today there is an all-out effort to present homosexualism as an acceptable life-style, approved by both God and man.

Part of the pressure for acceptance comes from the secular world, which has abandoned moral absolutes in favor of evolutionary science and humanistic philosophy. The *Humanist Manifesto II* (1973) declares, "Ethics is autonomous and situational," meaning that each person decides for himself what is right or wrong according to the situation. It also says, "Short of harming others or compelling them to do likewise, individuals should be permitted to express their sexual proclivities and pursue their life-styles as they desire." This of course is exactly the message of the Gay Liberation movement, which proclaims homosexualism as "a completely normal and satisfying option for sexual fulfillment."

To hear this from secular sources is not surprising. What might surprise us is to hear the *very same* message from the *religious* world today. In 1968 a new denomination, the Metropolitan Community Church (MCC) was begun just for homosexuals. Its distinctive "gospel" is that God accepts gays just as they are and does not require any change of life-style. As one MCC minister has said, "I'm a gay man and a minister. I expect to go home tonight to my gay lover with whom I have lived for thirteen years. Tomorrow I expect to preach to my congregation and to administer Communion to them. And I think God and I will feel quite good about it all." This group now has over 165 congregations and is seeking membership in the National Council of Churches.

Pressure groups exist within many mainline denominations, lobbying for full acceptance of gays and the ordination of practicing gay ministers. Examples are the Presbyterian Gay Caucus, the United Methodist Gay Caucus, and Dignity (a Roman Catholic group). In 1977 the delegates at the Disciples of Christ General Assembly rejected a resolution to condemn homosexualism as an alternate life-style for Christians.

How can this be happening in Christendom itself? Largely because a great many denominational leaders no longer accept the Bible as God's Word and thus pay no attention to its teaching on homosexualism. As one minister of the MCC has said, "We have learned not to get hung up on the Bible."

The most distressing thing, however, is that a growing number of *Bible-believers* have begun to defend the homosexual life-style, claiming that the Bible never really condemns it! Following the lead of others, they proceed to reinterpret every relevant Bible passage to say that only *certain kinds* of homosexual acts are wrong. They conclude that responsible, loving gay relationships are acceptable to God.

It is my conviction that faithful Christians must respond to these voices with a resounding NO! The Bible does *not* condone homosexualism, but condemns *all* homosexual practices in no uncertain terms. The rest of this chapter will examine this Biblical teaching, and will show that the attempts to reinterpret it so as to justify a gay life-style are futile.

I. *Sodom's Sin*

The name of Sodom has long been identified with homosexual behavior, and the horrible condemnation to which the city was subjected has been taken as proof of God's abhorrence of this sin. The Bible gives a glimpse of Sodom's character in the incident recorded in Genesis 19.

When the two angels who came to Sodom entered Lot's house, the men of the city gathered at the door and said, "Where are the men which came in to thee this night? bring them out unto us, that we may know them" (verse 5, King James Version). The word *know,* as we have seen, sometimes means "have sexual intercourse." That is the common understanding of this verse. The New American Standard Bible translates it, "that we may have relations with them"; the New English Bible says, "so that we can have intercourse with them." God destroyed Sodom and her sister cities for more reasons than one (Ezek 16:49, 50), but one reason was that they "indulged in gross immorality and went after strange flesh" (Jude 7).

Some defenders of homosexualism argue that Sodom's sin was merely *inhospitality.* The mob's request to "know" the two angels is taken to mean that they just wanted to "get acquainted" with them; however, their manner was rude and inhospitable. That hardly warrants such severe punishment as befell the city, though. Also, Lot's offer to send out his daughters in place of the angels shows that he knew the mob's intentions were sexual.

Others argue that the sin of Sodom was the intent to commit violent rape against the two angels, and that this is not a condemnation of loving homosexual relationships. It is true that this one incident was a case of attempted homosexual rape, but Lot's offer of his daughters shows that it was not just rape that was considered wicked, but the homosexual aspect of it as well. Also, we must not think that Sodom was destroyed for this episode alone. Jude 7 says that "Sodom and Gomorrah and the cities around them" were made an example of God's wrath because they "indulged in gross immorality and went after strange flesh." The episode recorded in Genesis 19 is characteristic of a perverted life-style existing in the whole area. The reference to "strange flesh" is a euphemism for the homosexual activity common in all the cities. The issue is not whether the activity was violent or "loving"; the point is that it was "strange flesh."

II. *Clear Condemnation*

In addition to the Sodom incident, the Bible contains clear condemnation of homosexualism in both testaments. The law of Moses has two prohibitions: "You shall not lie with a male as one lies with a female; it is an abomination" (Lev 18:22); "If there is a man who lies with a male as those who lie with a woman, both of them have committed a detestable act; they shall surely be put to death" (Lev 20:13). These commands are in the same context as prohibitions of incest, occultism, and bestiality. These and other things are the abominations that defiled the Canaanites and caused God to bring judgment upon them, says Moses (Lev 18:24-30).

To those who say, "That's the *Old* Testament," we need only to refer to Paul's explicit condemnation of homosexualism in the New Testament: "Do not be deceived; neither fornicators, nor idolaters, nor adulterers, nor effeminate, nor homosexuals, nor thieves, nor covetous . . . shall inherit the kingdom of God" (I Cor 6:9, 10). Also, "The law is not made for a righteous man, but for those who are lawless and rebellious, for the ungodly and sinners, for the unholy and profane, . . . for murderers and immoral men and homosexuals and kidnappers . . . , and whatever else is contrary to sound teaching" (I Tim 1:9, 10).

Paul's strongest condemnation of homosexual activity is in Romans 1:18-32. Here he says that those who deliberately reject the knowledge of the true God and go after false gods will become deeply mired in every sort of depravity, as God abandons them to their perverted desires. Of all the sins mentioned here, the one singled out for explicit and extended treatment is homosexualism. Here are Paul's words:

> Therefore God gave them over in the lusts of their hearts to impurity, that their bodies might be dishonored among them. . . . For this reason God gave them over to degrading passions; for their women exchanged the natural function for that which is unnatural, and in the same way also the men abandoned the natural function of the woman and burned in their desire towards one another, men with men committing indecent acts and receiving in their own persons the due penalty of their error (verses 24, 26, 27).

These passages from Moses and Paul should be sufficient to show us the mind of God concerning homosexual activity. "But wait!" says the revisionist; "these verses do not condemn *all* homosexual relationships. Only certain kinds are ruled out, i.e., only idolatrous, lustful, exploitive, and perverted homosexual acts are meant here. These passages say *absolutely nothing* about loving relationships between those who are homosexual by nature."

Along this line some contend that Leviticus and perhaps even the Pauline passages are not speaking of homosexualism as such, but rather the prevalent pagan idolatry that often involved homosexual acts as part of worship. Since these would be along the line of casual, promiscuous encounters, this type of activity was condemned. But these advocates of homosexuality see no explicit repudiation of acts between homosexuals "within a covenant of loyalty and tenderness."

In reply, we must point out first that there is actually *no real evidence* that ritual homosexualism was a widespread practice among the pagans. Also, we must insist that the passages themselves do not qualify or limit the types of activity condemned. They refer to homosexual acts *as such.* The most natural interpretation of such unqualified prohibitions is that *all* homosexual activity is included.

Some would claim that the very terms used by Paul in I Corinthians and I Timothy refer to some very specialized types of acts, including perhaps cult prostitution and the exploitation of young boys. The fact is that the terms in question (translated "effeminate" and "homosexuals" in the New American Standard Bible) are quite general terms and were used for all kinds of homosexual acts. There may be one distinction between them. The word for "effeminate" literally means "soft" and was used to refer to the passive partner in a liaison; the word for "homosexuals" more specifically referred to the active partner. Together they include all kinds of homosexualism. (Though these terms were limited to males, Romans 1:26 shows that female homosexualism is also condemned.)

III. *Natural or Unnatural?*

We focus our attention now on one further attempt to avoid the clear meaning of these passages. It centers on the teaching of Romans 1. It appears that Paul here is condemning homosexual acts as *unnatural.* However, some try to interpret this as referring *only* to heterosexuals who engage in homosexual acts just for perverse thrills. It does *not* include, they say, loving homosexual relationships between persons whose *natural inclination* is toward those of the same sex. For such people, *homosexualism is natural;* hence it is acceptable to God. (God is not pleased, of course, with homosexual lust or promiscuity—just with serious, loving commitments.)

This is no doubt the most common argument for some kind of divinely-approved gay life-style, i.e., *this is just the way God made some people.* "God made me, and God doesn't make mistakes" is an oft-heard gay slogan. The Bible is said to be totally silent about such "constitutional homosexuality," as it is called, and the silence is interpreted as *consent.*

How do we respond to this? Is this really what Paul means by "natural" and "unnatural" in Romans 1? Our answer is definitely NO. The point is that homosexual acts are unnatural not because they go against a particular individual's "nature," but because they contradict the very nature of sexuality as God originally created it.

The key to this understanding lies all the way back in Genesis 1—3, in the fact of the creation of one male and one female to represent the divine norm for sexual relationships. Any deviation from this norm is just that—*a deviation.* It is *not* normal, but is the result of *sin.* Many just do not acknowledge the effects of sin upon nature. They assume that "whatever is, is good." But this is not the case. The entrance of sin into the world (Gen 3) had a broad effect upon the universe, corrupting and perverting nature on a wholesale basis. For instance, physical death is not natural among human beings, but it has become our condition because of the first sin.

The homosexual condition must be understood in the same way. The condition itself is not natural, but is present because of the distortion of human nature by sin. This does not mean that an individual who has such a condition is sinful *as such.* It *is* sinful, however, to give in to this unnatural condition and engage in homosexual acts. It may be the case that the Bible does not mention the homosexual condition, but it does mention the acts and condemns them without qualification.

Sometimes an appeal is made to the fact that Jesus in the Gospels does not say anything about homosexualism. This is supposed to show that there is nothing wrong with it. Christ's silence on the issue is taken as carrying more weight than Paul's actual words. As one MCC preacher said, "If homosexuality is an abomination, why didn't Jesus address it? The only apostle that did was Paul, an egotistical self-centered individual." Another MCC minister adds, "Paul does not speak for Jesus Christ. There is nothing in the Gospels about homosexuality."

This is an example of how easy it is to distort the purpose of both Christ and the Bible. It is a rejection of the unity and authority of the Scriptures. Christ did not say anything about homosexual behavior for two reasons. One, the purpose of His life was not to provide a guide for holy living; He came to die and rise again. Second, He did not *have* to speak on the subject, *because* it *is* dealt with elsewhere in the Bible. ALL Scripture is inspired of God and profitable for correction and instruction in righteousness. Paul's statements are just as authoritative as anything in the Gospels.

In fact, it is *not true* that Jesus said *nothing* relevant to this issue. His positive teaching on heterosexual marriage as the norm established by creation (Matt 19:1-12) confirms the fact that homosexual acts *and* the homosexual condition are unnatural.

Is it possible for one who is a constitutional homosexual to change? Studies indicate that it is possible in a large number of cases, and I Corinthians 6:11 suggests that Christ can heal this condition in the context of the Christian life: "And such were some of you; but you were washed, but you were sanctified. . . ." This will not be automatic and may involve a terrible struggle, in which the Christian community should give support and encouragement. If one finds himself unable to change, he will then, as a Christian, resolve to remain celibate, just as many heterosexuals must do because of certain circumstances. Is it worth the cost and the effort? Yes. The *gay* life is traded for a life of real *joy* in Christ. It is much more than an even exchange.

5

DIVORCE AND REMARRIAGE

During my student days I worked one summer for a small factory in a Kentucky town. One of my single co-workers, whose life-style could well be described as sensual and impure, announced one day that he was planning to be married. When I asked him if he realized the seriousness of this step, he replied airily, "I thought I'd give it a try. If it doesn't work out, we'll just get a divorce." How typical, I thought, of the way so many people today view marriage and divorce. They take it about as seriously as buying a motorcycle: "I wonder what it's like to have a motorcyle! I think I'll try one. If I don't like it, I can always sell it."

What a deplorable attitude! As we have seen, marriage is the most important of all human relationships. If this is so, then the breaking up of a marriage must be one of the most tragic events in human experience. Christians must realize this, and must diligently guard against absorbing the world's nonchalance toward divorce.

There are many facets of the divorce problem; our discussion in this chapter will be limited to the Biblical teaching on the subject.

What is God's will with regard to divorce and remarriage, as revealed in Scripture?

I. *Divorce*

The original purpose for mankind did not include divorce at all. It is God's reluctant concession to a fallen world. The Mosaic law permitted divorce (Deut 24:1) for a reason ("indecency") which the Jews understood in a variety of ways. Jesus' comment on this law shows God's attitude on the subject: "Because of your hardness of heart, Moses permitted you to divorce your wives; but from the beginning it has not been this way" (Matt 19:8). In fact, says Malachi 2:16, God hates divorce!

In the New Testament era the world is still fallen and hearts are still hard; therefore God still permits divorce today. According to His revealed Word, however, there are only two circumstances in which it is a valid option: sexual immorality, and desertion by an unbelieving spouse.

A. *Sexual Immorality*

Adultery is generally seen as a valid "Biblical ground" for divorce wherever such a ground is acknowledged at all. Actually the term used in Scripture is not the specific word for adultery, but the more general term referring to any sort of sexual immorality (often times translated "fornication"). Jesus said, "Whoever divorces his wife, except for immorality, and marries another commits adultery" (Matt 19:9). See also Matthew 5:31, 32; Mark 10:11, 12; Luke 16:18.

Exactly what is meant here by the use of the term *immorality*? Some give it a very narrow interpretation in this context. They say it refers not to adultery but to pre-marital unchastity. If the evidence for such is discovered during the engagement period, this is then grounds not for divorce but only for breaking the engagement. Once a marriage has occurred, divorce as such is *never* justified. But this is not a proper understanding of Jesus' statement. He is talking about *divorcing* one's *wife,* not breaking an engagement. The Old Testament passage which started the discussion (Deut 24:1) refers to a marriage situation, not just a betrothal.

Others have tried to make the word *immorality* too general in meaning. Rushdoony says that it does not necessarily refer to sexual sin at all, but can refer to a wife's general insubordination toward her husband and toward God's created order for the home (*Institutes of Biblical Law,* pp. 404-411). But this view does not do justice to the use of the term both in the New Testament and in the Greek Old Testament. It almost always has a definite sexual connotation.

Both of the above extremes must be rejected. The term refers to sexual immorality on the part of a husband or a wife. The general term is used in order to include such sins as incest and homosexualism. These are acts of sexual infidelity and give grounds for divorce just as adultery does. Certainly the term *includes* adultery, as suggested by its use in I Thessalonians 4:3. Here the Christian is told to abstain from immorality; in the next verse he is told to "possess his own vessel in sanctification and honor." To "possess one's own vessel" most likely means "to live with one's own wife." One should not be unfaithful to his own wife by engaging in immorality—i.e., adultery—with someone else.

The point is that sexual immorality, which in most cases would be adultery, is a valid ground for divorce.

A serious question is WHY? *Why* should adultery constitute a ground for divorce? Why is it such a serious sin? Why this, and not wife abuse, for instance? The answer lies in what we have already discussed about the nature of marriage and the role of sex in marriage.

It will be remembered that marriage is the uniting of two lives on every level, both physical and spiritual. It means the joining of two bodies, but more significantly it means the joining of two hearts in a mutual covenant of exclusive love. This includes a vow to be sexually faithful to one's spouse. The sexual union itself, by God's intention a powerful uniting force, serves to strengthen the total bond between a husband and wife.

The act of adultery strikes, then, at the very jugular of the marriage relationship. First, the very act designed to unify husband and wife is used to join one of the spouses to a third party. Sex by its very nature *unites* (I Cor 6:16). Thus an unfaithful husband (for instance) is not just "having a little fun on the side." He is forming a union between himself and an outsider, thereby destroying the integrity of the union with his wife. Thus the physical link in the marriage bond is severed.

Second, the act of adultery is a violation of the *spiritual* covenant in which each spouse vows to keep himself exclusively for the other. In other words, sexual immorality in marriage is much more than a physical act. It is like a cauldron of acid in which the spiritual ties of promise, commitment, and trust are dissolved.

Thus adultery has the force of breaking the marriage bond on one side, and the offended spouse is free to dissolve the union from his or her side as well, via divorce. (We may note that divorce is not *necessary* in such a case, but it is *permitted.* If the original union can be saved without the final step of divorce, via repentance and forgiveness, this is infinitely preferable. "Remarriage" to one another is not necessary in such a case, but a recommitment is in order.)

B. *Desertion by an Unbeliever*

Many understand the Bible as giving only one valid ground for divorce, i.e., sexual immorality. Others see an additional ground, revealed later through Paul in I Corinthians 7:10-16, namely, the desertion of a believer by an unbelieving spouse. I believe the latter view is correct.

When the church began to spread through the pagan world, a new kind of situation began to arise. Often, just one partner in an existing marriage would be converted. What should the believer do in such a case, since this would now be an "unequal yoke"? (II Cor 6:14). In I Corinthians 7:10, 11 Paul reminds us of the teaching of Jesus, recorded in the Gospels, that *neither* partner should initiate a divorce. This had already been revealed during Jesus' earthly ministry; thus Paul can call it not just *his* instruction, but *the Lord's* (verses 10, 11).

But then Paul proceeds to give some inspired teaching to *add to* what was already known. He addresses the problem of a converted spouse married to an unbeliever. In this situation, he says, the believer *still* should not initiate a divorce (verses 12-14). *But,* if the unbeliever himself sues for divorce, in effect deserting the believer, then the divorce is valid. Verse 15 says, "Yet if the unbelieving one leaves, let him leave; the brother or the sister is not under bondage in such cases." The words "not under bondage" probably refer to the marriage bond, i.e., the bond no longer exists.

Let us not misunderstand Paul's distinction between *Christ's* teaching and his *own* teaching (verses 10-12). Paul is not placing his teaching on a lower level of authority. The distinction is between what Christ had already revealed *personally,* and what He is now revealing by the Spirit of God through Paul (verse 40). Revelation through an apostle is just as authoritative as Christ's own direct teaching (John 16:12-15).

This teaching, then, does not contradict Matthew 19:3-9, but complements it. It is *new* teaching in light of a new situation. We should note also that it is a very limited and specific teaching. It applies *only* to a case where a believer is married to an unbeliever, and the unbeliever (*not* the believer) initiates the divorce.

Thus there are two Scriptural grounds for divorce. If divorce occurs on either of these grounds, the marriage bond is totally dissolved, both *morally* and *legally.* This marriage no longer exists.

II. *Remarriage*

After a divorce occurs, is remarriage permitted for either or both of the parties involved? Some would say no, not even if there was a Biblical basis for the divorce. They contend that the Bible gives no such freedom. The divorce is treated as only a separation, and I Corinthians 7:11 is applied: if a wife *leaves,* "let her remain unmarried, or else be reconciled to her husband."

In my judgment this is not a correct understanding of the Bible. First Corinthians 7:11 seems to refer to a separation or perhaps to a divorce without a Biblical ground, not to a Biblically-permitted divorce. The crucial statement is Matthew 19:9. "Whoever divorces his wife, except for immorality, and marries another commits adultery." The phrase "except for immorality" is best understood as applying *both* to divorce *and* to remarriage. Except in the case of immorality (to which the inspired apostle adds the case of desertion), both divorce and remarriage are wrong. But if either immorality or desertion occurs, both divorce and remarriage are permitted. What must be understood is that a valid, Biblically-based divorce truly severs the marriage bond. The original marriage is dissolved, morally and legally. *It no longer exists.*

In such a case, which party is permitted to remarry? The answer is *both* parties, the "guilty" as well as the "innocent." Traditionally it has been felt that only the latter should have this right, and that the guilty partner does not deserve to have it. Such a feeling is understandable; but it is not based on Scripture, which specifies no such limitation. The guilty party in a divorce has sinned and must answer to God for his sin, but once the divorce has become final he is just as unmarried as the innocent party.

What about remarriage in the case of a divorce which has *no Biblical ground?* The key to this problem is this: no matter what the civil government says, unless there is a Biblical basis for the divorce, *the marriage still exists in God's sight* until such time as a Biblical ground (such as adultery) occurs. In this case the first person to engage in sexual relations, whether in a new marriage or before, commits the sin of adultery and actually dissolves the old marriage. From this point on the situation becomes the same as in the case of a valid divorce. Both parties are accountable for any sins that have brought them to this point; but once the adultery has occurred, the first marriage no longer exists. Any subsequent marriage, including the first remarriage, is a valid marriage.

This leads to a consideration of two rather common notions in relation to divorce. One is the idea that anyone who remarries after a non-Scriptural divorce is "living in sin" or "living in adultery." The other is the contention that a person who is illicitly remarried (however this is understood), if he wants to please God, must leave the person he is living with and return to his original spouse.

Both of these ideas, however, are wrong. The fact of the matter is this: following a divorce, no matter what its cause, *any remarriage is a valid marriage.* It may have *begun* with an act of adultery, but subsequent sexual relations within the new marriage are *not* adultery. The new marriage is the *only* one that exists. No spouse in a remarriage can go back to his original marriage for two reasons. One, there *is* no original marriage to go back to. It no longer exists! Second, leaving (divorcing) the new spouse without a Biblical ground would be starting the problem all over again. It would be initiating *another* non-Scriptural divorce. Instead of solving the problem, it would only compound it.

One other question needs to be considered. What if a person enters into a non-Scriptural divorce while he is an unbeliever, and then becomes a Christian? Does this mean that he is free to remarry? After all, he is now a Christian, forgiven of all sins, with all things made new in Christ. Shouldn't he be able to begin anew, as if nothing had ever happened?

No. Not necessarily. True, all his *sins* are forgiven; but being married or unmarried is a state, not a sin. Becoming a Christian does not affect one's marital status. If the other spouse has in the meantime committed adultery or remarried then the new convert is free to remarry—but not as a result of his becoming a Christian. If both spouses have remained single and celibate, the marriage bond is still intact before God. *Becoming a Christian does not break that bond.*

We close with a few words about innocence, guilt, and forgiveness. It is no secret that a real stigma is attached to divorce, and a divorced person is often treated as a moral leper. Even the innocent partner is made to feel tainted somehow.

How can we avoid serious injustice toward divorced persons? First, we should remember that the innocent party in a divorce—at least as far as the divorce is concerned—is just that: *innocent.* There is no moral stigma either for the divorce or for a remarriage. Such a person should be received in full fellowship. There is no need for confession or forgiveness, since there is no guilt.

On the other hand, the *guilty* party in a divorce *has* sinned by committing the deed that severed the marriage bond. Thus he bears the blame for the dissolution of the marriage. In the case of a non-Biblical divorce, one can sin in two ways: (1) by causing the divorce to happen in the first place, and (2) by being the first to remarry (or commit immorality), thus actually breaking the marriage bond.

What should be done in the case of one who has sinned in relation to his divorce? First, the guilty person should acknowledge that he *has* sinned. He must not rationalize his sin nor excuse himself; he must call his deed by its rightful name: SIN. Second, he should *confess* his sin to God and to anyone else he has wronged (which may sometimes include a whole congregation), and ask forgiveness. Finally, the church must forgive the repentant sinner and restore fellowship. (Forgiveness and fellowship do not automatically entail fitness for service. It may be *inexpedient* for some fully forgiven Christians to hold offices of leadership.)

Often the most serious problem in this connection is not the unwillingness of the church to forgive, but the refusal of the guilty person to admit that he has done anything wrong. He wants the church not only to accept *him,* but also to accept his sinful *deeds* as right. This we cannot do. But we can and *should* accept the *person* who repents and resolves to "sin no more."

6

MALE AND FEMALE ROLES

Thoughtful minds have always been impressed with the order of the universe—its natural laws, its predictability and regularity, the symmetry between solar systems and atoms. Spiritual eyes have marveled at a similar order in the moral realm—God's commandments, their universal relevance, their harmony with man's well-being.

At the heart of the moral order of the universe is the principle of authority. God has ordained that order in human society shall be maintained via certain specified authority structures. These are family, state, and church. Within each of these spheres a relationship of headship and submission exists. In the church, every member must submit to the authority of the leaders (Heb 13:17). In the state, every citizen must submit to civil authorities (Rom 13:1). In the family, children must submit to their parents (Eph 6:1-3).

The question here is whether this same relationship of headship and submission also exists between husband and wife, and between men and women in the church. The following Scriptures seem to indicate that this is so:

"And he shall rule over you" (Gen 3:16).
"The man is the head of a woman" (I Cor 11:3).
"Let the women . . . subject themselves" (I Cor 14:34).
"Wives, be subject to your own husbands" (Eph 5:22).
"Let a woman quietly receive instruction with entire submissiveness" (I Tim 2:11).
Women must be "subject to their own husbands" (Titus 2:5).
"Wives, be submissive to your own husbands" (I Peter 3:1).

This array of passages appears to present a consistent testimony of the headship-submission relationship between men and women. This is usually referred to as the *hierarchical* view. It is also the traditional understanding of male-female roles.

But in recent years, under the influence of certain cultural currents (e.g., women's liberation), a different understanding of the male-female relationship has gained strength. Called the *egalitarian* view, it rejects the concept of headship and submission and argues for the full equality of men and women in the sense of a total absence of role distinctions. As might be imagined, this calls for a very different approach to the Bible passages cited above.

In this chapter I shall first summarize the egalitarian view, then I shall present the traditional or hierarchical view. I believe the latter to be the clear Biblical position on this issue. In a nutshell, men and women are equal before God in terms of dignity and worth, but they have separate and distinct roles to play in God's scheme of things, both in the home and in the church.

I. *Egalitarianism*

Those who reject all distinctions between male roles and female roles may be found among believers and unbelievers alike. Here we are concerned mostly with those who accept the Bible's authority and try to follow it. We want to see how they understand the Biblical teaching on this subject, especially the references to submission.

According to this view, God's eternal plan for men and women has been full equality. This is the way the first pair were created. That Eve was made to be a "helper suitable" for Adam (Gen 2:18) is interpreted to mean an equal partner. "Woman was created in every way the equal of man," say Letha Scanzoni and Nancy Hardesty in *All We're Meant to Be* (Word, 1974; p. 26). The relationship of submission is unnatural and exists only as a result of sin's presence in the world. The statement, "He shall rule over you," is part of the *curse* upon women (Gen 3:16), and nothing more.

Since Jesus came to remove sin's curse, it is assumed that He did away with the headship-submission requirements, along with all male-female role distinctions. The golden text for egalitarians is Galatians 3:28: "There is neither Jew nor Greek, there is neither slave nor free man, there is neither male nor female; for you are all one in Christ Jesus." This verse is called "the liberating vision," the "magna carta of humanity," and "the last word" (Paul Jewett, *Man as Male and Female;* Eerdmans, 1975; see pages 12, 142).

Evidence for a full interchangeability of roles is seen in the New Testament's references to a number of women who seem to be in positions of leadership. A few of these are Philip's daughters (Acts 21:9); Lydia (Acts 16:14, 15); Priscilla (Acts 18:24-26); and Phoebe (Rom 16:1, 2). In this last passage Phoebe is described by two terms which are interpreted by many as titles and are translated "deaconness" and "ruler" (Scanzoni, page 62).

But how do the egalitarians interpret the New Testament passages referring to submission? These are handled in a number of ways. For some the easiest solution is simply to say that the Bible is wrong at these points, and that Paul was guilty of chauvinism. (See Jewett, pages 112-119, 134-135.) Many are not willing to make this kind of statement, though, since it amounts to an attack on Biblical authority. Thus they seek other ways to interpret the references to submission.

One of the most common explanations is that the submissive role for women was an element of the secular culture of the Graeco-Roman world, as was slavery. The New Testament writers tolerated both, but pressed for a transcendent ideal, that of Galatians 3:28. Both submission and slavery are thus seen as relics of a dead culture, having no place in the true church today (Jewett, pp. 11-12, 137ff.).

Another common explanation is that the submission passages are dealing with special local problems in individual churches and thus are not meant to have universal application. For instance, Scanzoni and Hardesty speculate that the women in view in I Corinthians 14:34 and Titus 2:5 were new converts from paganism who kept disturbing the services by their endless stream of questions (pp. 69, 109-110). They also speculate that I Timothy 2:11, 12 refers to a local situation in which certain unqualified and bossy-type women were trying to take over. Thus "the passage seems directed at a particular situation rather than at stating a general principle." Indeed, "of all the passages concerning women in the New Testament, only Galatians 3:28 is in a doctrinal setting; the remainder are all concerned with practical matters" (page 71).

Finally there is the concept of "mutual submission," which is used to explain Ephesians 5:22. The key to this passage is supposedly verse 21: "Be subject to one another in the fear of Christ." Yes, the wife *should* be subject to her husband, but the husband should also be subject to his wife! The husband is the *head* of the wife (verse 23) only in the sense of *source*, i.e., the source of her strength and life. (See Scanzoni, pages 99-100.)

II. *True Headship and Submission*

I believe that the above summary of the egalitarian position is accurate and fair, though necessarily brief. I also believe that this egalitarian view is mistaken, that it is based on speculation and contrived "exegesis," and that the actual victims of culture-blindness are the egalitarians themselves; i.e., they have been seduced by a nonscriptural element of *modern western* culture (feminism, women's liberation) and are now trying to fit it back into the Bible.

The Biblical teaching on the relation between the sexes can be summed up in two concepts: (1) *equality* in terms of dignity and status before God; yet (2) true *headship and submission* in relation to one another, resulting in a clear-cut distinction of roles.

A. *Equality Before God*

The fact that men and women are equal in their worth and value before God can be seen in every part of the Bible. This equality is grounded in the fact that both male and female are created in God's image, and both are given dominion over the rest of creation (Gen 1:26-28).

We quite agree that the concept of a "helpmeet" or a helper suitable for Adam (Gen 2:18) does not imply a mere servant status for women. The account of Eve's creation in Genesis 2:18-20 shows that she was not just another animal to be ruled over, but was the equivalent of Adam himself, made to rule alongside him. She was a "helper of the closest possible rank'' in their shared task of subduing the whole physical universe (Gen 1:28). The managerial ability of a good wife is praised in Proverbs 31:10-31.

Since both male and female are in God's image, both are equally capable of a personal relationship with the Creator. Both can worship and pray and serve. Likewise, both can rebel against God, and both must bear their responsibility for sin. On the Judgment Day sinners of both sexes will stand equally condemned, just as Adam and Eve shared the original condemnation (Gen 3:16-19).

But most important, both male and female share alike in the salvation provided by Christ. When it comes to receiving and enjoying the benefits of redemption, all distinctions are irrelevant. God is no respecter of persons. There is no group that receives privileged treatment in the distribution of saving grace; no special group stands closer to Christ than any other.

This is the point of Galatians 3:26-28. *Each individual*—whether Jew, Greek, male, or female—is equally a child of God (none are just nieces or nephews or stepchildren). Each person becomes a child of God by the same means, ''through faith in Christ Jesus'' (there is no privilege of birth or wealth). Each individual comes under the blood of Christ in the same humbling act, baptism (there is no front door as distinct from the servants' entrance). ''There is neither Jew nor Greek, there is neither slave nor free man, there is neither male nor female; for you are all one in Christ Jesus.'' The woman does not have an inferior status; she is ''a fellow-heir of the grace of life'' (I Peter 3:7).

B. *Distinction of Roles*

This concept of equality before God does not rule out role distinctions when men and women are considered in their relation to each other. The equality of Galatians 3:28 *cannot* be taken as negating the headship-submission principle stated so clearly elsewhere in the New Testament. There is absolutely no conflict between them.

Furthermore, it is totally unfounded to claim that only Galatians 3:28 has any abiding doctrinal relevance, while all references to submission applied only to particular first-century circumstances and need not be taken seriously today. This can easily be refuted by reading I Peter 3:1-7. Here Peter says, ''Wives, be submissive to your own husbands so that even if any one of them are disobedient to the word, they may be won . . . by the behavior of their wives'' (verse 1). The command to be submissive is *not* given just to wives of unbelievers, as Scanzoni and Hardesty allege (page 93), but to wives in general—*some* of whom *may* have unbelieving husbands. In verses 5 and 6 Peter shows that submission was not just a passing phenomenon of first-century culture, as he cites the example of Old Testament women who were ''submissive to their own husbands.'' The prime example to imitate is Sarah, who ''obeyed Abraham, calling him lord.''

So here is a reference to submission which is general in application, not limited to a cultural or specific situation. And an important point is that the passage concludes in verse 7 with a reference to equality: ''You husbands likewise, live with your wives in an understanding way, as with a weaker vessel . . . ; and grant her honor as a fellow-heir of the grace of life''! Thus equality and submission are presented side by side without a hint of contradiction.

How does this apply in the home? Both I Peter 3 and Ephesians 5 are relevant here. In each passage the wife is commanded to be subject to her husband, and in Ephesians 5:23 the husband is called ''the head of the wife, as Christ also is the head of the church.'' This means that the husband is to assume the role of *leader* in the family. It does not mean that the wife simply fades into the background, meek and mute, and takes orders. It means that she *allows* her husband to take the lead while she assists and contributes in every way possible.

The husband's role as head of the wife does not give him the right to boss and to browbeat and to be domineering. This is specifically forbidden in the comparison with Jesus' headship over the church in Ephesians 5. Christ's headship must unquestionably be understood in the sense of lordship (see Eph 1:22; Col 2:10), but it is a lordship tempered by love. The husband likewise must love, nourish, and cherish his wife (Eph 5:25-29). As Peter says, he must live with her ''in an understanding way, as with a weaker vessel.'' The wife should not be considered a ''weaker vessel'' in the sense of a cheap plastic cup, but rather as a delicate porcelain vase—to be treated with honor and care.

The attempt to interpret Ephesians 5 in terms of *mutual* submission and thus egalitarianism does not square with the total teaching of the Scriptures. Verse 21 does say to ''be subject to one another,'' meaning, of course, in every way that submission is appropriate. In other words, respect the various orders of submission and authority that God has established.

For example, it is proper for wives to be subject to their husbands; therefore let Christian wives be submissive (Eph 5:22). But this can *not* be turned around; this is not the point of verse 21. Husbands are not to submit to their wives any more than Christ submits to the church.

For another example, children should obey their parents (Eph 6:1-3). Should parents also obey their children? Obviously not.

Again, let slaves be obedient to their masters (Eph 6:5-8). Should masters also take orders from their slaves? No. (By the way, not *all* slavery is evil—only *involuntary slavery.* Thus the New Testament references to slavery are not necessarily culturally limited.)

Finally, how does the principle of submission apply in the church? I Timothy 2:11-13 sums it up: "Let a woman quietly receive instruction with entire submissiveness. But I do not allow a woman to teach or exercise authority over a man, but to remain quiet. For it was Adam who was first created, and then Eve." This shows that women should not be in roles of general leadership in the church, since they are not to "exercise authority over" men. To make women elders and preachers is a violation of Scripture.

This also shows that women are not to teach men. Gifted women should exercise their talents by teaching children (at least their own) and other women (Titus 2:3-5).

Some try to distort this by saying that the word translated "exercise authority over" can mean "commit murder" and thus must be forbidding a *sinfully* domineering spirit in women and not leadership as such. For at least three reasons I must conclude that this is a mistake: (1) If this is what the word means, then why limit the prohibition to women? Such would be wrong for men, too. (2) The words for "exercise authority" and "commit murder" are *not* the same word. The former is used here, not the latter. See Moulton and Milligan, *The Vocabulary of the Greek Testament,* page 91. (3) Finally, the comparison with verse 11 shows that ordinary authority is what is forbidden, as compared with submission.

Others try to say this passage deals only with a limited local cultural situation. This is refuted by the passage itself, i.e., verse 13, where

Paul bases the submissiveness principle on the very order of creation: "Adam was first created, and then Eve."

But were there not women leaders and teachers in the early church? Yes, women could prophesy (Acts 21:9; I Cor 11:5); but this was a miraculous gift, not ordinary teaching. Priscilla did help her husband teach Apollos about Christian baptism (Acts 18:24-26); but this was private, not public, and we do not really know how much of a role Priscilla played in the explanation.

What about Phoebe? She was a *diakonos* (Rom 16:1), but the word can refer to a servant in general as well as to one holding the office of deacon. There is no basis for assuming it means "deaconness" in this verse. But even if it does, the office of deacon is *not* an office of authority in the New Testament, though it is often wrongly considered so today. The attempt to call Phoebe a *ruler* instead of a *helper* (Rom 16:2) disregards the context. Phoebe was surely not *Paul's* "ruler."

In short, there are no New Testament examples that violate the general principle of headship and submission in the church context.

A few general remarks may be made in closing. First, this divinely-established order puts a great responsibility on men, and a great many men have shirked their responsibility by not preparing themselves spiritually and intellectually for leadership in the home and the church. This is to their shame.

Secondly, the *principle* of headship and submission is universally valid, but it may express itself in different ways in different cultures. It may have to do with hair length or head covering (I Cor 11:1-7), or it may have to do with the type of clothing worn (Deut 22:5). Christians should definitely respect the cultural expressions of the principle, whatever they are.

Finally, the roles of headship and submission should not be confused with superiority and inferiority. The male is not superior, nor the female inferior. Equality of worth and dignity must not be forgotten.

7

WORK: JOB OR JOY?

A schoolteacher in the "Mary Worth" comic strip was discussing his work with a friend. The friend said, "I can't understand how anyone can accept the hassle teachers are getting today." The teacher replied, "Because it's my job! Work isn't meant to be easy. If it was, they'd call it 'fun,' not 'work'!"

When I read this, I was intrigued by the implication that if work were easy, we would call it "fun." This would change our way of speaking somewhat. "Bye, Honey, I'm off to fun." "Hello, Boss? I'm sick and can't come in to fun today." "What time will you be home from fun?"

I don't really suppose this will ever happen, because for most people work truly is at the opposite end of the spectrum from fun. The fact is that work is just not very popular today. The so-called "work ethic," which upholds the honor and dignity of honest labor, is being attacked by many. In some circles the honorable person is no longer the one who works, but the one who can figure how to get by *without* working.

Even among Christians there is an attitude crisis with regard to work. Many view it in a completely negative way, thinking that work is actually a part of the curse inflicted on man because of sin (see Gen 3:17-19). In any case work is regarded as drudgery and as boring and burdensome. There is very little job satisfaction.

Why does modern man have such a negative attitude? Basically, because he has lost the Biblical perspective on work. The solution is to regain this lost perspective and to begin to understand work in the light of God's Word. This will not necessarily convert our work into *fun,* but it will make it infinitely more meaningful and satisfying.

I. *The God-Dimension of Work*

The Bible describes work from three different perspectives: as it relates to God, to others, and to ourselves. The most important is the God-dimension. Work, like everything else we do, must be done to the glory of God (I Cor 10:31). This is true in two ways.

First, our work must glorify God as our Creator. Because we are created in God's image, we *must* work. It is a natural and necessary part of our lives. When we work, we are simply imitating our Maker, who is constantly working. Once when Jesus healed a man on the Sabbath Day, he was accused of breaking God's law. He answered, "My Father is working until now, and I Myself am working" (John 5:17). In a similar way we also can say, "Our Father works, and therefore *we* work."

This has been God's intention for man from the very beginning. It is true that the curse upon sin has affected our work, as Genesis 3:17-19 shows. But the human race was given work to do before sin entered the picture. Besides the specific task of tending the Garden of Eden (Gen 2:15), Adam and Eve and their offspring were given the job of subduing the whole earth (Gen 1:28). This continuing responsibility involves most of the professions, industries, crafts, skills, and services that provide employment today. When we "go to work," we are simply fulfilling our God-given mandate to subdue the earth—something that we are to do for the glory of the Creator.

In the final analysis work is not optional but is a moral necessity. We are created to work, and we are commanded to work. The fourth Commandment (Exod 20:9) contains this admonition: "Six days you shall labor and do all your work." Paul reminds us of this obligation:

"But we urge you, brethren, to excel still more, and to make it your ambition to lead a quiet life and attend to your own business and work with your hands, just as we commanded you; so that you may behave properly toward outsiders and not be in any need" (I Thess 4:10-12). Again he says, "If anyone will not work, neither let him eat" (II Thess 3:10). The wisdom of Proverbs condemns the slothful and lazy person (6:6-11; 26:13, 14).

But there is another aspect of the God-dimension of work. Through it we honor God not only as our Creator but also as our Redeemer. The Christian's job or occupation is one of the ways in which he fulfills his *main* calling, which is to bring glory and honor to the one who has saved us from sin.

Sometimes we think of our work in terms of *vocation,* a word which literally means "calling." As Christians we actually have *two* vocations or callings. Our primary calling is described in I Peter 2:9, which says, "But you are a chosen race, a royal priesthood, a holy nation, a people for God's own possession, that you may proclaim the excellencies of Him who has called you out of darkness into His marvelous light."

Christians, here is our true vocation: by His gospel God has *called* us out of darkness into His marvelous light! For what purpose? Simply this: that we should "proclaim the excellencies" of the one who called us! Our number-one responsibility, our primary goal, our main job in life is to bear witness to the one who saved us.

This means that *everything else* we do is subordinate to this principal vocation and is a means to it. What does this have to do with our work—our "other vocation," as someone has called it? As with everything else we do, our job or profession is one of the ways by which we seek to honor our Savior. We work not just to make money, and not just to help others; primarily we work *to proclaim the excellencies of God.* "Whatever you do, do your work heartily, as for the Lord rather than for men" (Col 3:23).

What implications does this have for our daily work? First, it will help us determine the *choice* of our occupation. Of course, there are times when we may not have a choice as to our work. When jobs are scarce, a person has to take whatever is available. Many of us, though, set out to pursue a particular career. The question is, what are the most important considerations in our choice of a career? For some it is family tradition (what did your father do?). For others it is money (what pays the most?). Still others look for convenience (what is available? what requires the least real work?). For the Christian, however, the most important factor is this: Where can I be of the most use to God? Where can I best proclaim His excellencies? What kind of job will permit me to have the most influence for Jesus Christ?

The answer will not be the same for everyone, but here are some guidelines that everyone can apply. (1) It should be obvious that any immoral or illegal occupation is out of the question. (2) Ordinarily the best kind of occupation will be one that allows the most contact with *people*, especially in situations where there is a real opportunity for influence. Examples are teaching, preaching, social work, and nursing. (3) One should choose an occupation that allows him to develop his abilities to the fullest, one that allows him to advance as far as possible within that particular sphere of influence. One should use his job to gain as much respect and recognition as possible—not to glorify himself, of course, but to provide a larger "pulpit" from which to proclaim the Savior's excellencies. (See Matt 5:13-16.)

A second way in which our primary vocation affects our daily work is that it motivates us to do our *very best,* no matter how ordinary or how exciting our job may be. Because we are Christians, the *way* we work reflects upon the one whose name we wear. When we do our best, we gain others' respect; and this reflects honor upon our Lord. Thus we should always do our job well in terms of quality, and we should give full measure in terms of quantity—a full day's work for a full day's pay. Shirking and doing sloppy work bring dishonor upon our Lord.

A third implication for our daily work is that we will actively seek to use our job or profession as an occasion for witnessing about our Lord. Up to this point we have considered factors that relate to witnessing in an indirect way: choice of occupation, quality of work. Here we are talking about direct witnessing to our co-workers.

On-the-job witnessing is not easy and may not always be possible. We must respect company rules and the employers' right to his employees' time. We must also respect a co-worker's right to privacy. That is, we should not abuse a "captive-audience" situation. If anyone listens to our testimony, it should be because he wants to, not just because he cannot leave his post. Testimony to an unwilling listener would be counterproductive anyway.

Probably the best use of the job situation is to cultivate friendships and to gain respect by doing quality work and by living a consistent Christian life. Further contacts can then be made after working hours.

Above all we must remember that our main vocation is proclaiming the excellencies of the one who has saved us. Each Christian must make a judgment as to the wisest use of his job toward this end. (See James 1:5.)

II. *The Neighbor-Dimension of Work*

Work takes on new meaning when seen in relation to God, but it acquires even more significance when seen as an expression of neighbor-love. The second most important commandment is "You shall love your neighbor as yourself" (Matt 22:39). Love for one's neighbor *requires* us to work, and it helps us develop the proper *attitude* toward our work.

The basic factor here is the interdependence of the members of a society. Self-sufficiency is a myth; we *depend* on one another in a great number of ways. This is especially true of work. In almost everything we do every day, we depend on the labor of hundreds, even thousands of others.

As I sit at my desk writing this paragraph, I am depending on those who made paper, pen, ink, lamp, desk, chair, cup, coffee, and reading glasses, among other things. If I take just one of these, the lamp, for example, I find that I depend on those who made the bulbs, shaped the metal, mined the ore, made the tools that mined the ore and worked the metal, made the wiring, provided the electricity, mined the coal that produced the electricity, transported the coal—the list seems endless, and this is just for one item!

In view of this tremendously large and complex network of interdependence, what *is* work? It is much more than "earning a living" or "employment." Work is the individual's personal contribution to the total system of mutual aid. It is doing one's part to sustain and improve society as a whole. It is what each of us does to bear his share of the load in an interdependent world.

This must not be limited to just one kind of work. The expression "the working man" usually has a much too limited connotation. Besides excluding working women, it is commonly used to refer only to manual or blue-collar labor, or only to union members. But work is a much broader concept than this. It includes blue collar and white collar, manual and mental, management and "labor," clock-punchers and salaried, skilled and unskilled, factory and office, crafts and professions, paid and unpaid. Each category makes its contribution to the general well-being; each is *work.*

This understanding of work has several implicatons for the individual. For one thing, it helps us see why refusing to work is a sin. A deliberate refusal to work is a refusal to carry one's share of the total load. Such a person is a parasite, a burden. He takes without giving. He lives off the work of others, but makes no contribution in return. This is a direct violation of the meaning of love.

This is why a person must work to support his family, too. (See I Tim 5:8.) It is a matter of love not just for the family members, but also for one's neighbors, who would have to support them otherwise.

This also shows the heinousness of welfare cheating. Welfare or unemployment compensation is not wrong as such, since many who *want* to work cannot do so for various reasons. But those who *could* work and choose not to, living instead off welfare or other government subsistence, are stealing from their neighbors. They are violating the basic law of neighbor-love. Paul says it well: "If anyone will not work, neither let him eat" (II Thess 3:10). (Note: this applies only to those who *will* not work, not to those who *cannot* work.)

There is another side to this. What if a person has so much money that he does not have to work? He then is not a burden on others. As I understand it, such a person still is obligated to work—to do something constructive for society—even if he does not need the money. We work *not* just for ourselves, but also for *others.* It is a matter of service, of bearing one's share of the load. *Love* requires us to do our share and not to shirk our responsibility. As Paul puts it, one should work "in order that he may have something to share with him who has need" (Eph 4:28). One need not work for money, of course. He may instead volunteer his time and abilities to a church or service organization.

Finally, an awareness of the neighbor-dimension of work should enable each individual to see his job or profession as truly meaningful and useful. The person who makes bottle-caps, for instance, can take genuine satisfaction in knowing that he has helped to meet someone's needs or made others' lives more enjoyable. The person who lays bricks can take pride in his work and be glad that he has helped others have a place to live or work or shop.

A Christian man once lamented that he felt he was wasting his life working in an automobile factory. I told him to think of the many people who depend on *his* profession in order to accomplish *their* own tasks: the minister who needs a car to visit the sick and the lost, the doctor who drives from office to hospital, the mailman who brings us our mail. He said he had never thought of it that way.

An article in a recent *Reader's Digest* disturbed me greatly. It was about a vascular surgeon named Joe Hill who performs delicate and life-changing operations—an admirable profession indeed. But the disturbing part of the article was the suggestion that only such glamorous and dramatic work is *useful.* The article says, "Joe Hill is a man with an opportunity rare nowadays. He gets to do useful things." More than money or fame, "the fact of being essential is what pleases Joe Hill," (Mark Kramer, "A Surgeon's Day," *Reader's Digest,* January 1980, page 74).

Sure, the surgeon's work is useful, and perhaps worthy of more acclaim than most other jobs. But *almost all* work is *useful.* What about the people who make Joe Hill's surgical instruments? What about the people who scrub the operating room floors? What of those who clean his patients' bedpans? It is totally false to imply that very little work is really useful.

III. *The Self-Dimension of Work*

Work relates to God and to our fellow man, and of course it also relates to ourselves. We *do* work for our own sake, too. For most of us, our work is the means of "making a living." It is the way we pay for the necessities of life.

Genesis 3:17-19 makes this connection between *working* and *living:* "Cursed is the ground because of you; in toil you shall eat of it all the days of your life. . . . By the sweat of your face you shall eat bread." It is possible that the very necessity of working in order to live is part of the curse brought about by sin. Our very life and existence depend upon work; we must sweat in order to eat. Perhaps this is what makes work into toil and drudgery and fosters our negative attitude toward it.

This aspect of the curse can be minimized when we see our work in the broader terms suggested in this chapter. When we do, it is no longer just a matter of self-survival; it becomes a means of *self-expression.* Through our work we express our power of creativity (like God); we express our joy and gratitude and praise to our Maker; we express our love for our fellow man.

John Stott comments on this self-dimension when he says that "work is intended for the fulfillment of the worker." He refers back to the fact that we are made in God's image. "Therefore our potential for creative work is an essential part of our God-like humanness, and without work we are not fully human. If we are idle (instead of busy) or destructive (instead of creative) we deny our humanity and so forfeit our self-fulfillment." ("Reclaiming the Biblical Doctrine of Work," *Christianity Today,* May 4, 1979, page 36.)

When we put work in its total positive perspective, seeing it in all its dimensions, it becomes a source of personal fulfillment and satisfaction. It becomes a joy, not a job. It becomes what God intended it to be, namely (in Stott's words), "the expenditure of manual or mental energy in service, which brings fulfillment to the worker, benefit to the community, and glory to God" (*ibid.,* page 37).

8

LABOR STRIKES

The question of the morality of labor strikes is a very emotional one, and I realize how difficult it is to consider it objectively. Labor strikes have been an accepted part of our culture for the entire lifetime of most or all who are reading this book. Many sincere Christians are union members and have participated in strikes. On the other hand, many have suffered mental, physical, and financial harm as the result of strikes. Thus we are bound to encounter strong opinions pro and con.

Our purpose in this chapter is to analyze the very concept of a labor strike in the light of Biblical morality. Here it is very important to remember that our final authority on all ethical issues is the Bible—not tradition, not feelings, not even American laws.

At the very outset we must recognize that certain particular kinds of strikes are immoral, regardless of what is concluded about the concept as such. For instance, striking contrary to a contracted agreement (e.g. violation of a no-strike clause) is wrong, since it violates truth and faithfulness—the very pillars of righteousness and order. Also, striking contrary to law is wrong, since we are commanded to obey civil laws (Rom 13:1). Civil disobedience, except in cases where obeying a law would require us to sin, is forbidden. Also, it should be obvious that acts of physical violence in connection with any strike are wrong. This includes destruction of property as well as harm to persons. Such acts are contrary to the general law of love, and to the sixth Commandment, the eighth Commandment, and Matthew 5:38-48 in particular. They are also contrary to civil law and thus are forbidden on that basis.

Another strike that is immoral is one with *unjust ends*. There is no question that labor strikes often seek just ends, but many times this is not the case. Selfish and greedy motives have driven many unions to seek unconscionable wage increases and unreasonable fringe benefits. For instance, a New York union went on strike when the city refused to grant their demands: a thirty percent wage hike, a thirty-two-hour work week, and six weeks' vacation after one year of service. Other unions have demanded—and received—a day off with pay when donating a pint of blood, two hours off with pay to deposit one's paycheck, and overtime pay for normal clean-up after work. As one observer has noted, a strike "is rarely employed to ensure justice to mistreated workers, but is used frequently to make well-paid specialists more affluent."

But what about cases where justice *is* at stake? What about strikes that *do* have a just goal? This brings us to an analysis of the very essence and concept of a labor strike. My firm conviction is that a strike by its very nature is contrary to the law of love and therefore is immoral. For those who would disagree, I would ask that a fair hearing be given to my arguments, and that all discussion be directed toward seeking God's will in this controversial matter.

I. *The Nature of a Strike*

Many ethical problems must be examined in terms of both *ends* and *means*. Sometimes the end may be morally right, but the method or means used to achieve that end may be morally wrong. In such a case we must remember a basic ethical principle: good ends *do not* justify bad means.

A labor strike is basically a means to an end. Whatever that end may be, our concern here is to analyze the exact nature of a strike as a means of achieving it.

Sometimes a strike is defined as a cooperative withholding of labor. One correspondent described it as the "work force withdrawing their labor to get the company to negotiate in a businesslike manner." In a sense this is true, but it is not the whole picture. A strike is much more than a mere "withholding of labor." It also involves misused *power* and one or more kinds of *violence.*

A strike is obviously an exercise of power. In a strike effort a union exerts its collective power in order to prevent the company from hiring replacement workers and to force it to make certain concessions. What kind of power is used to achieve these goals? It is neither the power of reason nor the power of moral persuasion. It is rather *coercion,* in which one group forces another group to enter an agreement against its will, *by the threat of or infliction of violence and harm.* A strike is essentially ineffectual without this basic ingredient of violence. The violence is not necessarily physical, though there is often plenty of that. Violence includes harm or injury of any kind, even if it is no more than financial harm to the company being struck. But the deliberate intent of *every* strike, by its very nature, is to cause or threaten *harm* as the means of gaining the desired ends.

II. *A Violation of Love*

When we see that the very purpose of a strike is to threaten or inflict harm, how can we possibly reconcile this action with biblical ethics? It sounds much more like the worldly principle of "might makes right," an approach to ethics which is very common but which is contrary to Scripture.

The final standard of all right action is the will of God, and God's will for humankind can be summed up in the word *love* (Matt 22:35-40). Every action must ultimately be tested against the standard of love. When labor strikes are thus tested, they fail miserably. They are in almost every respect a violation of neighbor-love.

How can one say he loves his neighbor when he deliberately sets out to *harm* him for personal gain? Let there be no mistake here. All harm and threats of harm in relation to a strike are against *people.* Harm may take many forms: loss of income, sales, education, fire and police protection, property, even life. But all such loss is *some person's* loss; it is harm against *persons.* We are not dealing just with abstractions: "the public," "management," "property." It is a *person's* wages that are lost when he cannot cross a picket line for fear of violence. It is a *person's* house that burns when fire protection is denied. These are persons we are supposed to *love.*

A strike violates love in several ways. First, it harms those who want to work but who would have to cross a picket line in order to do so. Those who do cross it are sometimes subjected to the most inhuman and unloving treatment: thrown rocks, eggs broken on their cars or houses, slashed tires, telephone threats, mean and vicious verbal abuse. Those who do not cross the line for fear of such harm are robbed of their wages. (Just this week TV news showed a union picket line at a midwestern company. Cars driven through the line were pelted with rocks by sneering strikers. Windshields were broken.)

A strike violates love because it *deliberately* harms the employer, whether this be a private company or the taxpayers of the "public sector." The basic reality in the former case is that the strike is intended to cause economic loss to the employer. By inflicting such loss through stopped production and sales, and by threatening to inflict still further loss, the union forces the employer to capitulate. The same is true of a strike against the public sector. By inflicting suffering on the public—loss of police protection, children deprived of education, garbage rotting in the streets—the union forces a settlement.

The truth has to be faced. The labor strike is usually *no different in principle* from criminal acts such as robbery and extortion. The dictionary definition of *extort* is "to wrest or wring from a person by violence, intimidation, or abuse of authority; obtain by force, torture, threat, or the like." God's word in I Corinthians 5:10; 6:10 condemns those who rob or plunder or seize someone else's goods by force. The word is translated as extortioners in the King James Version and as swindlers in the New American Standard Bible and the New International Version.

A strike violates love also in that it involves a total lack of concern for the impact of the extorted wage settlement upon consumers in general. Apart from the complex question of the role of such wage increases in inflation, we need only to stress the fact that the ones who actually pay the extorted wages and fringes are the consumers (or taxpayers, in the public sector). The employer has little incentive to hold out against a strike when he can simply pass the increased costs on to his customers in the form of higher prices.

This makes the labor strike a unique form of extortion. In an ordinary robbery the criminal puts a gun to the victim's head and says, "Give me *your* money or I will harm you." The labor union, however, says to the employer, "Give me the *consumer's* (or public's) money or I will harm you." When the employer yields he is in effect entering into a conspiracy. He becomes a party to inflicting suffering on the very one who has no voice in the matter: the consumer (public).

Jesus said, "Love your neighbor as yourself" (Matt 22:39). He blessed the meek and the peacemakers (Matt 5:5, 9). He said, "Do not resist him who is evil; but whoever slaps you on your right cheek, turn to him the other also" (Matt 5:39). We are taught to be content (I Tim 6:6-10). A labor strike simply cannot be reconciled with this teaching, nor with the whole Biblical picture of the Christian life.

III. *What About Justice?*

The question of workers' rights must still be addressed. There is no doubt that employees have suffered and in some cases may still suffer injustice at the hands of greedy employers. Unjust wages and working conditions, accompanied by a take-it-or-leave-it attitude, helped to spawn the labor movement in the first place. Such treatment by management is just as unloving and wrong as a labor strike and must be similarly condemned.

But what recourse do workers have to correct such grievances besides the strike? Is there a *proper* method of achieving and ensuring justice in the labor market? Yes. God has established such a means. It is the *civil government.* The very purpose of government is to make sure that justice is done. This includes protecting the rights of the innocent and punishing those who try to violate their rights. (See Rom 13:1-5; I Tim 2:1-4.)

When government is doing its job, it will not allow employers to exploit or endanger workers. This means that government does have some responsibility to see that fair wages are paid, and that safe working conditions are provided. (Whether it is fair and efficient in practice or not, the Occupational Safety and Health Act is not wrong in principle.)

A labor strike is in effect an attempt by private citizens to usurp the role of government. God has given the power of the sword (coercion) to civil rulers alone; individuals are *not* to take justice into their own hands. (See Matt 5:38-48; Rom 12:17—13:4.) But this is what is happening in a strike. The workers judge (correctly or not) that they are being treated unjustly; the strike is a means of correcting the alleged injustice by force. Let us press for a government that will live up to its God-given duties—one that will protect workers from unjust employers *and* one that will protect employers and the public from the coercive violence of labor strikes.

A second means for correcting injustice has been provided by God in Scripture. Whenever management is exploiting the workers, God's spokesmen are to sound a warning to those who would gain wealth at their workers' expense. "Behold, the pay of the laborers who mowed your fields, and which has been withheld by you, cries out against you; and the outcry of those who did the harvesting has reached the ears of the Lord of Sabaoth. You have lived luxuriously . . . you have fattened your hearts in a day of slaughter" (James 5:4, 5). Those who withhold all or part of what their employees have earned should be warned that God will judge "those who oppress the wage earner in his wages" (Mal 3:5). See also Leviticus 19:13; Deuteronomy 24:14, 15; Jeremiah 22:13.

Conclusion

Can a Christian belong to a union? Yes, there is nothing wrong with belonging to a union *as such.* In practice, however, a union means little without the power of the strike. So anyone who opposes strikes on principle may have to face some difficult decisions. What should he do if his union strikes? I am convinced he should not support the strike or vote for it, nor should he *willingly* participate in it. For his own safety he may have to stay away from work during the strike, but he should respectfully decline to participate in any strike-related activities.

(There are other problems of conscience that some may have with regard to union membership. These include *compulsory* unionism, where one is forced to belong to a union—and pay dues to that union —for the privilege of working. Also included is the possible *misuse* of union dues, e.g., to support political causes and candidates contrary to the views of one who pays dues.)

A change of attitude toward labor strikes will be difficult for many, but I earnestly plead for an objective examination of the issue, and a prayerful study of it in relation to God's Word. The "American way" is not necessarily the *Christian* way, and it definitely is not the Christian way in this case. Let us have the courage to acknowledge it and to act accordingly.

9

LEISURE

Leisure suits. A man of leisure. At your leisure. A life of leisure. Leisure time.

Leisure is a word we use occasionally, but it is not easily defined. Exactly what is leisure time? Sometimes it is thought of as the opposite of work, but this is not accurate. In chapter 7 we saw that work involves whatever we do to sustain and improve society as a whole. This may include some activities, such as volunteer hospital work, that are done on one's leisure time. Thus work and leisure may overlap at some points.

Leisure is often equated with rest and recreation time, but this is not accurate either. Leisure includes these elements, but it is a much broader term and includes many other kinds of activities.

Leisure is best understood as all the time *not* spent at making a living, or providing for one's household, as I Timothy 5:8 puts it. The time necessary for making a living includes not only one's forty or so hours of vocational time, but time spent in many non-paying tasks such as house repairs, shopping, cooking, and general housework.

Leisure, then, is the time we can use as we choose once we have provided a living for ourselves and our families. Some formal definitions are "opportunities offered by freedom from occupations"; "the state of having time at one's disposal"; "time which one can spend as one pleases"; "free or unoccupied time." Some use the expression "discretionary time."

I. *Leisure as a Moral Problem*

The proper use of leisure is definitely a moral problem. Changing cultural patterns in the late twentieth century have intensified the problem considerably. More and more time is being shifted into the leisure category by such factors as shorter work weeks, longer vacations, speedier transportation, earlier retirement, and longer life. Urban and suburban living leaves young people with large amounts of free time. Also, more money for leisure and more options for spending it complicate the problem even more.

The big temptation—the big danger—is to think of leisure time as "our very own," which we can use totally as we please without any restrictions whatever. *This is a serious error in thinking!* In a God-created universe, *everything* belongs to the Creator, including us and our time (Ps 24:1, 2). God is the Lord of all (Acts 10:36), and He is the Lord of time. We no more "own" our time than we own our possessions; we are only stewards of that which the true Owner allows us to use.

The question is, has God laid down any restrictions that we His stewards must take account of in deciding how to use our leisure time? Yes, definitely! These restrictions are mostly general in nature, but they will help us to make specific choices if we conscientiously apply them.

A. *God's Glory Is First*

Before going into further detail about the use of leisure, we need to remember a few general principles from God's Word that apply to *everything* we do. First, the primary goal of our life as a whole and of every single activity in it is to bring glory and honor to God. "Whether, then, you eat or drink or whatever you do, do all to the glory of God" (I Cor 10:31). Jesus said that we should first—above all else—seek God's kingdom and righteousness (Matt 6:33). The word *kingdom* basically means kingship, lordship and honor. Thus Jesus is saying that whatever else you may have in mind, *be sure* that everything you do honors and glorifies God.

This is getting down to basics, down to the question of your ultimate goal or highest good in life (your *summum bonum,* as the philosophers say). Just what is the most important thing in the world to you? What means more to you than anything else? What is your underlying philosophy of life? The answer is this kind of question is probably revealed in how you use your leisure time!

The *hedonist's* main concern is personal pleasure, and his free time is used mainly in seeking it. This does not necessarily mean immorality. Indeed a hedonist is a hedonist not because he seeks immoral pleasures, but because his main interest in life is pleasure. His leisure time is spent on a steady diet of fun and games. "Eat, drink, and be merry" is his motto. Every spare moment is stuffed with TV, video games, spectator sports, bowling, boating, and partying. Most of these may be innocent or even useful in themselves, but they reveal a hedonistic, selfish mind-set when they dominate one's leisure.

The *altruist's* goal in life is more noble, namely, to serve others. A person who really cares for others and wants his life to be of service to mankind will be inclined to use his leisure hours to do good deeds for neighbors and shut-ins, to be active in a service organization, or to do volunteer work of some kind. Such things are of course very commendable; and when compared with hedonism, the altruist's life-style is much to be preferred. One must remember, though, that serving others is still not the *highest* good. When these things dominate, e.g., when one's involvement in a lodge or club crowds out his church life, then God is not being honored.

The *Christian's* use of leisure time will be determined by the words of Jesus. God's kingdom and glory must come first. God has the primary claim on our lives. This does not exclude service to neighbors or even personal pleasure, but it does make them subordinate to the main goal. This affects not only the amount of time spent on each kind of activity, but also the nature of the activities engaged in for service or pleasure. For instance, in our choice of entertainment (e.g., the choice of a movie), we must ask, "Will my doing this in some way dishonor God?"

B. *Time Is Precious*

A second general principle that must be kept in mind is that time is valuable and precious; we don't have any to waste. Ephesians 5:16 and Colossians 4:5 exhort us to *make the most of our time.* Other translations say we should redeem the time, make the most of every opportunity, or make the best use of time. This shows that the availability of leisure time is a tremendous opportunity, and the use of it is a great responsibility. How to use leisure hours is no small consideration.

"Idle hands are the devil's workshop," as someone has said. That is, idleness puts one in a situation that can easily degenerate into some wicked activity. But we need to see that idleness *itself* is a victory for the devil. To waste time, to pass the hours doing nothing, constantly to escape into mindless, fruitless, pointless diversions is to fail in our stewardship of one of God's greatest gifts, time itself.

C. *What Will People Think?*

A third principle is that in all things our lives must set a good example for others and not cause them to stumble. The things we do should lead others toward God, not away from Him. Jesus said, "Let your light shine before men in such a way that they may see your good works, and glorify your Father who is in heaven" (Matt 5:16). Some things that we ourselves may be strong enough to handle will have to be avoided to keep weaker brethren from stumbling. "But take care lest this liberty of yours somehow become a stumbling block to the weak" (I Cor 8:9).

In other words, we must always think of how our leisure-time activities are going to impact on the minds of others. This may have special application to our choice of entertainment.

D. *Money Counts, Too*

A final principle that must be remembered is that we must be good stewards of our *money.* Even if we can justify the time spent on certain activities, excessive cost may prohibit them. For instance, exercise is important, and water-skiing may be a good and wholesome exercise, but traveling to the Bahamas in January just to water-ski may be poor stewardship of money. It is also easy to go overboard in spending on such things as hobbies, eating out, and home entertainment (e.g., video games).

II. *Aspects of Leisure*

Deciding how to use leisure time is something each of us must do for himself, keeping in mind the general principles just discussed. We want to be as conscientious as possible in allotting our time to those who have claims upon it. In this section we shall see that above all *God* has certain special claims on our leisure; also *others* have claims upon us; and finally we must save some time for *ourselves.*

A. *Time for God*

Actually, *all* our time is God's time, and we must use it all according to His will. There are certain activities, though, that are directed toward God in a special way; and these must have top priority as we arrange our leisure time. Private devotions and public worship head the list. "Closet prayer" is a daily necessity (Matt 6:6), and assembling together is commanded (Heb 10:25).

A Christian's church life does not end with a single assembly on Sunday. Fellowship with other believers is natural and needed and will bring us together for various church functions. Evangelistic calling and other calling also are needed. Those who teach must spend time in preparation; much work is involved in being an elder (I Tim 5:17) or deacon (Acts 6:1-6).

God does expect us to give priority to the work of His kingdom! Under the Old Covenant God sent the prophet Haggai to rebuke Israel for neglecting His temple. He had brought them back from Babylonian captivity around 536 B.C., and they began with enthusiasm to rebuild the fallen temple in Jerusalem. But their zeal waned, and they left the work half-finished for years while they went about their own affairs. Haggai shamed them by saying, " 'Is it time for you yourselves to dwell in your paneled houses while this house lies desolate? . . . Go up to the mountains, bring wood and rebuild the temple, that I may be pleased with it and be glorified,' says the Lord" (Hag 1:4, 8).

What sort of leisure activities are we today putting above our responsibilities to Christ's church? TV? Sports? Lodge meetings?

Camping? May the words of Haggai 1:7 shake us up: "Thus says the Lord of hosts, 'Consider your ways!'" Unless we are making time for God first of all, our other leisure activities become empty and vain.

B. *Time for Others*

Our leisure time must include time for others. This begins with time spent with family members. Husbands and wives must be sure to leave quality time available for one another. The same is true of parents and children. Providing for one's own (I Tim 5:8) may begin with material necessities, but it does not end there. Children need personal expressions of love and times of informal instruction.

As we get older we must not forget to set aside time for aging parents. "Honor your father and your mother" (Exod 20:12) does not cease to apply just because we no longer live in our parents' houses.

Time for others will also include volunteer service, at least occasionally. "So then, while we have opportunity, let us do good to all men, and especially to those who are of the household of the faith" (Gal 6:10). This is an especially good form of leisure for teens and retirees. A good Biblical example is Dorcas (Acts 9:36-42).

C. *Time for Self*

Finally, it is legitimate and even necessary to have some leisure time for oneself. This falls into several categories, which often overlap.

Rest. Personal leisure time must be used first of all to rest. This includes time for adequate sleep. The Gospels portray Jesus as occasionally taking time to rest. Once He told His disciples, "Come away by yourselves to a lonely place and rest a while" (Mark 6:31). See Matthew 14:13; 15:21.

The Bible pictures rest from labor as a blessing (Ps 23:2, 3; Matt 11:28, 29). In fact, good stewardship of life demands it. The pressure of unrelieved work can be destructive both physically and mentally. The value of vacation time is more and more appreciated just to provide needed rest.

On the other hand, too much rest is not good either. The Bible condemns slothfulness (Prov 6:6-11; 26:13-16). "Behold, these are the wicked; and always at ease" (Ps 73:12).

As long as we avoid the two extremes of workaholism and sloth, restful leisure is good.

Recreation. Some time spent just in playing or having fun is also appropriate. Some people have the idea that the Bible says it is wrong to have fun, but this is a grave mistake. Ecclesiastes 3:4 says there is "a time to weep, and a time to laugh; a time to mourn, and a time to dance." God "richly supplies us with all things to enjoy" (I Tim 6:17). Jesus attended feasts (Matt 11:16-19; John 2:1-10).

Thus periodic recreation or entertainment or amusement is certainly permissible. There is nothing necessarily wrong with watching TV, going to a movie, attending a ball game, playing tennis, or reading science fiction.

This aspect of personal leisure, however, is open to the possibility of many abuses and grave sins. We must be very cautious in our choice of entertainment, taking into account at least four factors. One is the *proportion* of leisure time spent simply on entertainment. Overindulgence in spectator sports, TV, or video games makes us guilty of idleness or wasting time. A second factor is the *cost* of entertainment. Are we exercising good stewardship? A third factor is the *motive* for a particular activity. Are we guilty of escapism—shirking responsibility, putting off more important things? The last consideration is the *character* of the entertainment. Unfortunately much of what passes as entertainment today is at best unwholesome and often just plain evil. How can a Christian attend a movie or read a magazine that mocks Biblical standards and glorifies immorality? How can he listen to song lyrics that incite to sinful lust?

Certainly we have a responsibility to ourselves and to others in our choice of recreation. We must above all be sure that it is truly creative—that it re-creates us and builds us up and strengthens us. Anything that is degenerating or mind-corrupting must be rejected.

Delight. One writer identifies delight as a distinct aspect of personal leisure. This seems to be an appropriate way of describing those activities in which we want to experience something for the pure delight and joy it gives us. Included here are aesthetic experiences: enjoying the beauty of art and music, and especially delighting in the wonders of God's creation. See Psalm 8.

Self-improvement. Finally, some leisure time may be spent in doing things to improve our bodies and minds. Physical exercise is important to good health and should be a part of one's routine. This may be combined with recreation if the exercise is something enjoyable, such as swimming or racquetball. Mental stimulation through reading or continuing education is also profitable.

Again we remind ourselves of the ever-growing opportunities for leisure and of our Christian responsibility to be good stewards of our leisure time. Addison Leitch has asked the key question: "Will the expansion of leisure be a degenerating experience or a creative one?" By the grace of God and a will truly submitted to Him, we can make it the latter.

10

PROPERTY

The private ownership of property is a universal fact of life. Practically everyone has something he can call his very own. It may be something quite meager and basic, such as an article of clothing or a string of beads. Or it may be a large ranch or a manufacturing business.

While most of us fall somewhere between these two extremes, the fact remains that we *do* own property or possessions, and will probably continue to accumulate more. We should want to know what the Bible says about owning things, especially since a number of serious ethical problems are related to this subject.

I. *The RIGHT To Own Property*

Property has been defined as "that dominion which one man claims and exercises over the external things of the world, in exclusion of every other individual." We must ask whether anyone has the *right* to claim such exclusive dominion over things—the right to possess, to use, to enjoy, and to dispose of them as he sees fit.

Most of us have never questioned our right to own property of all kinds, such as clothes, automobiles, houses, land, cows, tools, farm machinery, and grocery stores. The Fifth Amendment of the U.S. Constitution specifically guards the right to private property against unjust seizure, but in general the Constitution just takes this right for granted. We usually assume that it is one of our "natural rights."

This assumption has not gone unchallenged, however. In the course of religious history a number of groups, such as the Shakers, have attempted to set up communal societies in which all property is held in common instead of by individuals. Some have claimed that this was the practice of the early church: "And all those who had believed were together, and had all things in common" (Acts 2:44); "and not one of them claimed that anything belonging to him was his own; but all things were common property to them" (Acts 4:32).

A more formidable challenge to the concept of private property comes from the modern economic systems of socialism and communism, especially the Marxist variety. These systems do not oppose all private property, but they generally exclude the private ownership of the means of production and distribution of goods, e.g., farmland, factories, railroads, and retail stores. In theory such things as these are supposed to be owned by everyone together; in fact they are owned and operated by the government.

A considerable number of contemporary churchmen, Protestant and Catholic alike, have begun to support this aspect of Marxism. This is seen in the anticapitalist stance of many theologians, and in their support for Marxist-type revolutions in third-world countries. See, for example, Jose Miranda's *Marx and the Bible* (Maryknoll, NY: Orbis, 1974), in which the first chapter is entitled "Private Ownership Under Challenge."

A. *Sanctioned by Scripture*

How does the Bible approach the subject of private property? First of all, contrary to communal and communistic theory, it sanctions and protects the right of private ownership. The eighth and the tenth Commandments affirm and protect this right. "You shall not steal" (Exod 20:15) is God's commandment for us to respect the property rights of others. "You shall not covet your neighbor's house . . . or anything that belongs to your neighbor'' (Exod 20:17) specifically affirms that our neighbors, as individuals, have the right to claim ownership of personal belongings.

The Bible also sanctions private property when it states that leaving an inheritance is good: ''A good man leaves an inheritance to his children's children'' (Prov 13:22).

Jesus' parable of the laborers in the vineyard assumes that the vineyard has an owner (Matt 20:1, 8). He puts these words in the owner's mouth: ''Is it not lawful for me to do what I wish with what is my own?'' (Matt 20:15).

Peter described the property of Ananias and Sapphira in similar language: ''While it remained unsold, did it not remain your own? And after it was sold, was it not under your control?'' (Acts 5:4). This is important because it shows that the early Christians were not *required* to give up their private property and practice communal living (or communism); they *voluntarily* sold certain possessions and gave the money to the needy because of the emergency situation following Pentecost. (The Christians had all things in common in the sense that they considered whatever they owned as being available to meet the needs of the whole group.) Ananias and Sapphira did not *have* to sell their property; it was theirs to dispose of as they chose. Even after selling it, they did not *have* to give all the money to the apostles; it was still under their control. Their sin was in lying about the amount of money received for the property.

One thing to note is that various *means of production* are among the kinds of things approved by the Bible as legitimate private property. The tenth Commandment mentions the ox and the donkey—the equivalent of farm machinery. In Jesus' parable of the laborers (Matt 20:1-16) the vineyard was the possession of one man. An actual case of such ownership was that of Naboth the Jezreelite, a landowner who suffered injustice and oppression as the result of others' covetousness (I Kings 21:1-16). We should remember, too, that some of the apostles owned fishing boats and equipment (Mark 1:16-20; Luke 5:3-11).

B. *Bestowed by God*

Thus the Bible sanctions and protects the right to own property. But it also goes a step further, namely, it tells us the *origin* of this right. It is bestowed by God himself, who is the ultimate owner of everything by virtue of creation (Ps 24:1, 2). At the very beginning God stated His plan for mankind: "Let Us make man in Our image, according to Our likeness; and let them rule over the fish of the sea and over the birds of the sky and over the cattle and over all the earth" (Gen 1:26). Thus the Creator himself gives to mankind the gift of *dominion* over the resources of the earth.

C. *A Qualified Right*

One other point should be noted. The right to own things is real, and it is God-given; but is is also *qualified.* It is not an absolute, unlimited right. God has given us dominion, but not sovereignty. Here are some of the qualifications the Bible places on property ownership.

a. We must recognize that *God* is the primary and absolute owner of everything, even those things we rightly call our own. Psalm 24:1 says, "The earth is the Lord's, and all it contains, the world, and those who dwell in it." God says in Job 41:11, "Whatever is under the whole heaven is Mine." This applies to the houses we live in, the shoes on our feet, the food in our refrigerators, and the money in our bank accounts. We may have deeds and titles in our names, but it all belongs to God.

b. This means that we must see ourselves as *stewards* of the things we own. We cannot use our possessions only as *we* see fit; we must use them in accordance with God's instructions. We must use them not just to please ourselves, but to please God. We must use them only in such ways as bring glory to God (I Cor 10:31). Using one's television set to stir fleshly lusts, for instance, is a betrayal of stewardship. So is the use of one's paycheck to gamble, get drunk, or buy indecent records. "It's my money; I can spend it any way I want to" is *never* true.

c. We must be very careful to guard against *materialism.* That is, we must not allow the ownership of things—including the desire and the effort to acquire them—to dominate our lives. Jesus tells us emphatically that one's life does not consist of his possessions (Luke 12:15). In Matthew 6:19-34 He teaches us that the accumulation of material things must not be the goal of life. When making money and owning things become the most important part of our lives, we are worshiping Mammon (that is, riches) and not God (Matt 6:24). Thus Paul says that greed or covetousness is the same as idolatry

(Col 3:5), and he warns us not to fix our hope on the uncertainty of riches (I Tim 6:17).

Some churchmen have carried this Biblical warning against materialism to the extreme of suggesting that possessions *as such* are dangerous. They cite Jesus' statement in Luke 18:24, 25: "How hard it is for those who are wealthy to enter the kingdom of God! For it is easier for a camel to go through the eye of a needle, than for a rich man to enter the kingdom of God." I Timothy 6:9, 10 is also cited: "But those who want to get rich fall into temptation and a snare and many foolish and harmful desires which plunge men into ruin and destruction. For the love of money is a root of all sorts of evil, and some by longing for it have wandered away from the faith, and pierced themselves with many a pang." In referring to these passages, Ronald Sider speaks of the "deadly danger of possessions"; he says that "possessions are positively dangerous." (*Rich Christians in an Age of Hunger;* Downers Grove: InterVarsity, 1977; pages 120, 122).

There definitely are dangers associated with the things of this world, whether one is thinking in terms of much or little. But we should be careful not to go to the extreme of implying that it is wrong to own things. Possessions as such are not evil or dangerous. Even Sider recognizes that "they are not innately evil" (*ibid.,* p. 125). What is wrong is to put the pursuit of money or property ahead of everything else, to hoard this world's goods, to use them selfishly, to trust in them instead of in God. As Paul says, the *love* of money—materialism—is the root of all sorts of evil, not the money itself.

d. Those who have "the world's goods" must be ready to share them with those who are in need (I John 3:17). God allows us to own possessions so we can use them in serving others. He commands us to work and to earn money in order that we "may have something to share with him who has need" (Eph 4:28). Those who have much must "be generous and ready to share" (I Tim 6:18). This will not be difficult if we develop the attitude toward our possessions described in paragraphs b and c above.

e. Finally, ownership of property is allowed and blessed by God as long as we *acquire* it in a proper manner. This will be discussed in the next section.

II. *The BASIS of Ownership*

Granted that I have the right to own property as such, the next question is this: what gives me the right to claim ownership to this *particular* watch, or horse, or automobile, or farm, or twenty-dollar bill? Does it matter *how* I come to possess the things I own? Of course it does!

The primary consideration is the matter of justice. Practically everything is already claimed as the property of some individual or group or government. By what right may I claim that an item no longer belongs to someone else but now belongs to me? How may I acquire property or goods or money without doing injustice to another person?

A. *Unjust Ownership*

We must recognize that the transfer of ownership by unjust means is one of the major social and moral evils. The Bible forbids it, and a large part of civil legislation is designed to prevent it. It is generally known as theft or stealing, and is specifically forbidden by the eighth Commandment: "You shall not steal" (Exod 20:15). As Paul says, "Let him who steals steal no longer" (Eph 4:28). Thieves are listed with other sinners (I Cor 6:10) and keep company with Judas (John 12:6).

The more obvious forms of stealing do not tempt most of us: mugging, breaking and entering, armed robbery, looting, graft, embezzlement, rustling, using counterfeit money, even shoplifting. But what about more subtle forms of theft? How many of us have gained money or goods—

by underpaying helpers or overcharging customers?
by shirking or loafing at work?
by pilfering from Mother's purse?
by not returning a borrowed book?
by substituting inferior materials in a building project?
by falsifying a welfare claim or a food stamp application?
by falsifying an income tax form or an insurance claim?
by duplicating copyrighted music?
by making personal long distance calls on a company phone?
by permanently "borrowing" something from office or shop?
by lying about the condition of a car when trading it in?
by neglecting to pay the rent or debts incurred?
by riding a bus without paying the fare?
by sneaking into a theater or out of a restaurant?
by threatening harm or violence through a labor strike?

by taking a towel or a sheet from a motel room?
by taking silverware from a restaurant?
by performing unnecessary repairs on an automobile?

How many of us can truly say that everything we own has been obtained by just means? No wonder Martin Luther is reported to have said, "It is the smallest part of thieves that are hanged. If we are to hang them all, where shall we get rope enough?" Let us make sure that everything we obtain becomes ours by legitimate means.

B. *Just Ownership*

What, then, are the legitimate bases for property ownership? Basically there are two, a primary one and a secondary one. The primary basis for claiming ownership to something is *work*.

The Bible is clear in tying property ownership to work. God's original gift of dominion over the earth was conditioned on the commandment to *subdue* it (Gen 1:28). In this brief mandate lies the divine authorization for such work as farming, fishing, mining, manufacturing, and research. Through his involvement in such work, each man earns the right to own a portion of the creation.

Proverbs 13:11 sums up the whole issue in a nutshell: "Wealth obtained by fraud dwindles, but the one who gathers by labor increases it." The same wisdom is found elsewhere in Proverbs: "Ill-gotten gains do not profit. . . . Poor is he who works with a negligent hand, but the hand of the diligent makes rich" (10:2, 4). "He who tills his land will have plenty of bread. . . . The hand of the diligent will rule" (12:11, 24). "The soul of the sluggard craves and gets nothing, but the soul of the diligent is made fat" (13:4).

The New Testament echoes this relation between work and ownership: "Let him who steals steal no longer; but rather let him labor, performing with his own hands what is good, in order that he may have something to share with him who has need" (Eph 4:28). Paul states this in a negative way in II Thessalonians 3:10: "If anyone will not work, neither let him eat."

This truth is given a specific form in the teaching that *workers deserve their wages.* The Old Testament principle, "You shall not muzzle the ox while he is threshing" (Deut 25:4), is cited in the New Testament as referring also to human labor. Paul uses it to argue for the propriety of receiving wages for the work of ministry (I Cor 9:1-12; see I Tim 5:17, 18). In the same context he refers to this principle as it applies to other occupations: "Who at any time serves as a soldier at his own expense? Who plants a vineyard, and does not eat the fruit of it? Or who tends a flock and does not use the milk of the flock? . . . The plowman ought to plow in hope, and the thresher to thresh in hope of sharing the crops" (I Cor 9:7, 10).

Jesus makes this point in these words: "The worker is worthy of his support" (Matt 10:10). Paul states the same principle in Romans 4:4 (with a spiritual application): "Now to the one who works, his wage is not reckoned as a favor but as what is due." In these statements the key words are *worthy* and *due.* These are words expressing justice; there is a just and proper connection between work and wages.

The teaching that work is the primary basis for ownership (even of the food that keeps us alive—II Thess 3:10) is a death blow to the welfare mentality. As we have already noted, if a person *cannot* work even though he is willing, it is not wrong for him to accept the charity of others. The welfare mentality, however, is something entirely different. This is the attitude of a person who assumes that the government, or "society," or "somebody" *owes* him a living—even if he chooses not to work. Such thinking as this is erroneous, sinful, and dangerous to the well-being of society.

It should be noted that acquiring something by means of *purchase* or *trade* is the same as acquiring it by work, since in the transaction we are using something already obtained by our work (usually money). Someone has described money as "coined life"; we may also think of it as coined labor.

(Parenthetically we may note that "crimes against property" are often dismissed as being relatively insignificant when compared with "crimes against persons." In many ways this is a false distinction. Insofar as one's property has been acquired by his own labor, that property is a part of himself. If a man works twenty hours and uses his wages to buy a radio for his automobile, then whoever steals that radio commits a crime against the person—he steals twenty hours of the person's life.)

Thus when the workman receives his paycheck, he is receiving what is truly his own—if he has truly given an honest day's work for his day's wages. Likewise, when a farmer sells his crop or a writer sells a story, the money he receives is truly his own. Then when he trades this money for food, shoes, a house, or a plow, what he buys is his own by right.

We should also mention another basis for property ownership, i.e., by means of a *gift*. Though this is secondary to work, it is indeed a legitimate way to own things. It includes the transfer of ownership by means of inheritance, which Scripture sanctions: "A good man leaves an inheritance to his children's children" (Prov 13:22).

In view of the Bible's teaching concerning property, we should not feel guilty for owning possessions that have been acquired legitimately and that are being used properly. Let us remember, though, that property rights are granted by God, and the particular items that we own are gifts from God (James 1:17). This being true, how can we fail to obey the words of Proverbs 3:9, "Honor the Lord from your wealth"?

11

CAPITALISM

Capitalism is the name given to the economic system with which Americans are most familiar, *socialism* being the principal modern alternative. Though technically a mixture of the two, our system is more capitalistic than socialistic. We also call it the *free enterprise* system. This refers to freedom from government intervention. It means that the production, buying, and selling of goods are matters of industrial initiative and mutual agreement, and are not determined or regulated by the state.

Capitalism has been under attack for over a century and a quarter, at least since Karl Marx and Friedrich Engels published the *Communist Manifesto* in 1848. Many nations have switched to a socialistic economic system, some voluntarily and some under the duress of Communist dictatorships. Those that have not become socialistic, such as the United States, are under increasingly heavy pressure to do so.

This pressure comes in many forms, but here we will focus only upon the so-called ethical case against capitalism. The argument is that capitalism, in and of itself, is immoral. Some of those who press this argument are non-Christians, and some are Christians. Among the latter, some are liberal and some are conservative. The conservative opponents of capitalism argue that it is inconsistent with the Biblical principles of love and justice.

What does all this have to do with Christians today? After all, what can just an average citizen do to change the economic system under which he lives? Very little, if you happen to live under a dictatorship. But if you live in a democracy, where you have the opportunity to vote for those who make the laws, as well as to influence their thinking, then you can definitely have a part in determining the prevailing economic system.

The key issue is the role of government in controlling or regulating the economy. This is one of the main points of difference between political parties, between liberal and conservative politics, and between candidates running for public office. Some tend more toward increased government control, that is, socialism; some are more in favor of free enterprise and less government interference in the economy, that is, capitalism.

This issue is very important to each one of us. If capitalism is inherently anti-Biblical and immoral, then we should be making every effort to elect lawmakers who will change our system. We should be trying to influence the present officials toward a more socialistic stand. And, according to some, we should be encouraging the socialistic revolutions that are occurring in other countries, especially those of the third world.

On the other hand, if capitalism is *not* the villain that some say it is, if it is not immoral as such, then we will probably be a bit more hesitant to join the world-wide slide toward socialism. We may even find that there are good Biblical reasons, as well as pragmatic ones, for preferring capitalism over socialism.

In any case the first question to ask in deciding this issue is, What does the Bible say? This takes precedence over everything else. We must be careful never to defend (or oppose!) a particular position on any issue just because it is "the American way." The question is, Is it the *Christian* way?

I. *Three Basic Systems*

A. *Capitalism*

First we must give a brief description of each of the three main economic systems, beginning with *capitalism*. The capitalistic system is based upon the private ownership (as opposed to state ownership) of the means of producing marketable goods. This includes such things as land, resources, tools, machinery, and buildings—anything used in the production of other goods.

Capitalism is also known as the *free market system,* meaning that the market is free from state planning and control. Goods are exchanged on the open market, with the law of supply and demand being allowed to determine *what* is produced as well as the *price* for which it is sold. In the final analysis the consumer determines the market, since what the consumer can buy or will buy is what will be produced.

B. *Socialism*

The basic alternative to capitalism is *socialism,* which is the economic system in which the government plans and controls the market. This usually involves what is called the *public* ownership of the means of production, which means only that the government owns them. A state planning agency determines what is produced and the prices for which the products are sold.

There are two basic forms of socialism. One is the *Marxist* type, in which the economy is controlled by a totalitarian dictatorship. All production and economic policy are simply decreed by those in power; the people in general have no voice in choosing the plan or the planners.

The other type is democratic socialism. In this system the economy is still planned and controlled by the government, but the people are free to choose their government (and therefore their economic planners) in free elections. They also may freely criticize the existing government and form opposition parties.

As one observer puts it, these two types of socialism agree on who owns the means of production, namely, the state; but they disagree on who owns the state.

C. *Mixed Economy*

The third kind of economic system is not a pure alternative to the other two but is actually a combination of them. Thus it is called a mixed economy. In such a system the means of production are privately owned, but the government intervenes to regulate the production of goods, prices, and/or the distribution of income. A mixed economy will be more like capitalism or more like socialism, depending on the *degree* of state intervention, but conservative parties usually argue for less control while liberal parties demand more.

This system is also known by other names, such as interventionism and social market capitalism. It is the system which actually exists to some degree in most so-called "capitalist" countries, including the United States.

Does all this really matter? What is at stake? For one thing, the freedom to own productive property, such as a farm or grocery store or small business. For another thing, the freedom to use this property according to one's own choice. For another, the freedom to shop in stores stocked with an unbelievable variety of goods in unbelievable abundance—unbelievable, that is, to people who live in many socialist countries. Another thing at stake, of course, is the question of justice. This leads to the next point.

II. *Criticisms of Capitalism*

Michael Novak observes, "Throughout the world, capitalism evokes hatred. The word is associated with selfishness, exploitation, inequality, imperialism, war." (*The Spirit of Democratic Capitalism;* New York: Simon & Schuster, 1982; p. 31) Some critics argue that it is merely irrational, i.e., that as a system it is self-contradictory and unworkable. Others argue that it is absolutely wicked and inherently wrong. Here we will be discussing only the latter type of criticism.

The key word is *justice.* Criticism begins with the fact that capitalism allows the private ownership of the means of production. This fact, it is said, leads to all sorts of violations of justice. It causes selfishness and greed on the part of the owners (that is, "capitalists"), and allows them to exploit those who work for them. It leads to a state of economic inequality in which some have more than others; this is seen as unjust. The argument is that capitalism *always* causes such injustice; only socialism can avoid it and bring true justice.

We will now examine these criticisms in more detail.

A. *The Process*

The first aspect of capitalism that is attacked is the *process* by which goods are produced and sold. This process is said to be immoral because it revolves around the concept of *profit*. What keeps capitalism going is the profit motive, which in and of itself is immoral because it causes exploitation and injustice.

Consider the following example. Mr. C has an idea for a product that he thinks will be desirable to consumers, e.g., a soap that floats. He begins manufacturing it and eventually owns a small factory that employs ten workers, each of whom is paid $10,000 per year. Other costs (raw materials, machinery, depreciation, marketing, etc.) bring the total cost for marketing 400,000 bars of soap per year to a total of $180,000. Each bar of soap sells for fifty cents, for a total of $200,000. This leaves Mr. C with a net profit of $20,000.

Now according to the critic, this process has produced injustice in three ways. First, the capitalist has not been fair to himself. The pursuit of profit engenders selfishness and greed in his own heart, and he becomes motivated by purely selfish interests rather than love. This would be eliminated, we are told, if profit were eliminated and the government controlled the process.

Second, the capitalist exploits his workers. The laborer is paid only so much, but the product he makes is sold for much more than the cost of his labor. This surplus (i.e., profit) winds up in the capitalist's pocket, thus cheating the worker out of what is rightfully his.

Third, the buyer or consumer is exploited in a twofold way: the capitalist's relentless pursuit of profit means he has to pay more for the product than he should, and he is often seduced by clever advertising into buying unnecessary things.

B. *The Result*

A second kind of criticism of capitalism is directed toward the *result* of the process described above. The critic asserts that capitalism produces a state of economic and social *inequality*. Some people will ultimately have more wealth than others, sometimes much more. This has the effect of dividing society up into classes, alienating one group from another. All this is labeled *injustice,* and its alleged cause —capitalism—is severely condemned.

C. *The Solution*

The solution to all of this injustice, according to the critic, is government control of the means of production, or at least strong government regulation of production, sale of goods, and the overall distribution of wealth. This is supposed to eliminate or sharply limit profit and competition, and thus selfishness and exploitation. It is also supposed to result in full economic justice, which is interpreted to mean equality of ownership and wealth.

Many people believe this is the only position consistent with Christianity. See J. Philip Wogaman, *The Great Economic Debate* (Philadelphia: Westminster, 1977), pp. 133-135.

III. *Is Capitalism Christian?*

The charges against capitalism are very serious; and if they are valid, Christians should be the first to oppose it. In this last section we will examine these charges, and we will find that they are basically invalid.

A. *Private Property*

Anti-capitalists say that one of the basic evils of the system is the private ownership of property, especially the means of production. We have already seen in the last chapter that private ownership is not wrong but is sanctioned by the Bible. No further discussion is needed at this point.

B. *The Profit Motive*

Now we ask whether the profit motive is wrong as such. Does it always engender selfishness and greed? The answer is that it can, but not *necessarily* so. It is true that the love of money is the root of all sorts of evil (I Tim 6:10); thus the desire for profit may destroy a person spiritually and cause him to exploit others. But this is true not because money and profit are sinful as such, but because man's *heart* is sinful (Jer 17:9).

Greed cannot be blamed on the system; it arises in the heart and can corrupt *any* system, including socialism. Under socialism greedy officials and managers can (and often do) allot to themselves a disproportionate amount of goods, basking in abundance even if the majority goes hungry. Socialism also creates a situation in which man's greed leads to bribery and black marketing. It also exploits and justifies man's sinful tendency toward *envy,* where those who have less covet the possessions of those who have more and devise legal (if not necessarily moral) ways to acquire them. This is why socialism is sometimes called "the politics of envy."

Even in a capitalistic system, greed can cause the allegedly exploited workers to mount an organized labor strike, thus acquiring more money not by work but by extortion and violence. (See chapter 8.)

The point is that greed is not the exclusive sin of the capitalist, but is a constant danger for anyone under any system. Capitalists and socialists alike must guard against it, and it can be avoided by the grace of God under either system.

What about the charge that the capitalist's profit robs the worker of what is rightfully his own? This idea is not taken as seriously as it once was, because it is recognized that other things besides labor produce value in a product and thus account for the surplus value, e.g., the cost and maintenance of tools and machinery, the cost of selling the product, compensation for risk on the part of the owner (or co-owners, as in the case of stock-holders), and the owner's own work and expertise. Of course, an owner *can* exploit his employees (for example, as in "sweatshop" conditions and many migrant labor situations), but this is not inherent in the system.

What about the charge that the consumer is exploited? Again, it is possible, as in the case of false or manipulative advertising, or in the case of monopoly control and unchecked pricing of essential items. But again, these are not inherent in the system. Indeed, a free market system is the least exploitative of all, since its essence is a totally *voluntary* exchange in which each person trades something of lesser value to himself for something of greater value to himself.

One may say that socialism is far more guilty of exploiting the consumer (a category that includes everyone), since it sets artificial prices while usually limiting the amount, variety, and quality of the goods for sale.

The bottom line is the effect of sin on the hearts of individuals. Sinful capitalists are likely to take advantage of every opportunity to exploit others, but so are sinful socialists. "Changing the system" will not necessarily eliminate exploitation, since each system offers its own opportunities for injustice. The only solution is to change the hearts of men through the gospel of Jesus Christ.

C. *Inequality*

The final criticism of capitalism is that it results in an *unequal distribution* of wealth or property. Some (usually the capitalists) wind up with a greater share of the wealth than others. What shall we say about this?

First we acknowledge that this probably is the case. Some do tend to accumulate more than others under capitalism. The line of separation does not always fall neatly between owner and worker, however. As a result of high wages and stock ownership, many if not most workers enjoy a very comfortable standard of living. Still, a small percentage will be living in luxury. But this also happens in socialist countries, where the elite live in luxury while everyone else lives much further down the economic scale.

But this is not the heart of the criticism. The socialist says not only that economic inequality results from capitalism, but also that economic inequality is *wrong as such*. In the question of the distribution of wealth, the only just situation is equality of ownership. Justice demands it, and (says the Christian socialist) God demands it. Thus capitalism must be overthrown and socialism set up in its place. Socialism can provide equality by allowing everyone to own the means of production (via state ownership) and by making sure no one accumulates an excessive amount of wealth (via taxation and redistribution of income).

The basic question here is whether economic inequality is unjust as such, i.e., whether an equal distribution of property is the required ideal. In answering this question our final appeal must be made not to humanistic philosophies but to the Word of God. What does the Bible say? In essence, the Bible does *not* demand economic equality as a condition for justice; thus this criticism of capitalism is unfounded.

This fact is seen most clearly in the Biblical teaching on the subject of *wealth*. Wealth is understood as referring not just to the possession of goods as such, but to an abundant amount of goods. The basic fact is that God's Word does not condemn the possession of wealth or riches and does not demand that all wealth be redistributed until everyone has the same amount.

In the Bible, wealth in the hands of a righteous person is seen as a blessing from God. Psalm 112:1-3 says, "How blessed is the man who fears the Lord, who greatly delights in His commandments. His descendants will be mighty on earth; the generation of the upright will be blessed. Wealth and riches are in his house, and his righteousness endures forever." The wisdom of Proverbs tells us, "Honor the Lord from your wealth, and from the first of all your produce; so your barns will be filled with plenty, and your vats will overflow with new wine" (3:9, 10); "It is the blessing of the Lord that makes rich" (10:22); "Adversity pursues sinners, but the righteous will be rewarded with prosperity. A good man leaves an inheritance to his children's children" (13:21, 22). The Lord blessed the steadfast Job with great wealth (Job 42:10-12).

In carrying out his plan of redemption God used a number of persons who were wealthy. A chief example is Abraham, who "was very rich in livestock, in silver and in gold" (Gen 13:2). Likewise Isaac "became rich, and continued to grow richer until he became very wealthy." As a consequence he suffered injustice and oppression from his envious Philistine neighbors (Gen 26:12-15). Joseph of Arimathea, in whose tomb Jesus was laid, was a rich man (Matt 27:57).

As we saw in the last chapter, possessions and wealth are the natural fruit of diligent labor (Prov 10:4; 13:11; 14:23). Those who work harder deserve to have more.

The rich are warned that their wealth can become a stumbling block if they put their hope in it (I Tim 6:17), or boast about being rich (Jer 9:23), or forget that God is its source (Deut 8:17, 18). The wealthy young man whom Jesus told to sell all his possessions and give the money to the poor had apparently succumbed to covetousness, and Jesus was telling him the only way he was going to conquer this sin (Mark 10:17-22). Such drastic measures were not required of everyone, though. The fishermen-apostles did not dispose of their boats and fishing gear (Luke 5:3; John 21:3); the wealthy Zaccheus gave only one-half of his possessions to the poor, and Jesus praised him (Luke 19:1-9).

The rich are not condemned for being rich, but for other things. They are condemned for misusing their wealth. They are condemned for neglecting and oppressing the poor (see the next chapter). They are condemned especially if they have accumulated their wealth in an unjust way. Jeremiah 17:11 says, "As a partridge that hatches eggs which it has not laid, so is he who makes a fortune, but unjustly; in the midst of his days it will forsake him, and in the end he will be a fool." Amos condemns those who gain wealth by cheating the poor (5:11, 12; 8:4-7), as does James (James 5:1-6).

Those who have wealth are commanded to share with those who are *in need*, but only to supply what they need (as in the case of famine or other emergencies), and not in order to achieve economic equality. First John 3:17 speaks of helping a "brother in need." James 2:15, 16 says we should help a "brother or sister . . . without clothing and in need of daily food." Ephesians 4:28 commands us to "share with him who has need."

An example of this is the generosity of the early church. Many of the first Christians were visitors to Jerusalem who decided to stay there after being converted to Christ. Thus they were without homes, jobs, and possessions, and soon were lacking daily necessities. This is the reason why many of the new Christians sold some of their possessions—to share "as anyone might have need" (Acts 2:45; 4:35). It was a meeting of needs, not a complete redistribution.

As Paul traveled among the Gentile churches, he took "a contribution for the poor among the saints in Jerusalem" (Rom 15:26). He urged the church at Corinth to give in order to meet the *needs* of these saints, "that there may be equality" (II Cor 8:13, 14). The use of the word *isotēs* (equality) here should not be misunderstood as laying down a general principle of economics, a command to redistribute all wealth equally. The point is fairness or equality in the supplying of necessities, as shown by the reference to manna in the next verse (8:15). The term is used only here and in Colossians 4:1, where masters are told to grant their slaves "justice and fairness (*isotēs*)." Again the reference is not to total economic equality, but to a meeting of all needs.

True Biblical equality is equality before the law, equality of opportunity, equality in receiving justice. No one is to receive special treatment, whether poor or rich: "You shall do not injustice in judgment; you shall not be partial to the poor nor defer to the great, but you are to judge your neighbor fairly" (Lev 19:15). James reminds the brethren who tend to favor the rich that they are not to make such distinctions (James 2:1-4).

The main point is that the Bible does not equate economic inequality with injustice. It assumes that there will always exist those who "get along with humble means" and those who "live in prosperity," as Paul put it about himself, and it urges contentment while warning against covetousness (Phil 4:11-13; Heb 13:5). Thus this criticism of capitalism, that it results in inequality, is irrelevant.

Is capitalism an inherently immoral system? The answer is no. The accusations against it are without force. This does not mean that it is without flaws or that it is to be identified with Christianity. It does not mean that one must favor capitalism in order to be a Christian. It simply means that capitalism is fully consistent with Biblical teaching.

We close this chapter by raising a few questions about socialism and justice. Those who equate the two are basically assuming that economic equality—socialism's main goal—is the essence of justice. We have seen that this is not the case. Thus even if socialism achieves its goal, it does not necessarily achieve justice.

The fact is that socialism creates some injustices of its own. It takes away our full right to own private property. It also weakens the right of the worker to enjoy the fruit of his labor by taxing the productive worker for purposes of redistribution among the non-productive. In doing so it violates the principle that work determines ownership. Socialism also destroys our freedom to give to the poor voluntarily out of a glad and grateful heart. All of this is done through state intervention, which puts the government in the role of a violator of rights rather than a defender of rights.

12

POVERTY

Every day ten thousand people die of starvation.

Thirty percent of the world's population barely keep from starving.

One third of the world's children die of malnutrition or disease before their fifth birthday.

One hundred thousand children per year go blind for lack of vitamin A.

In a recent year twelve and a half million people lived as refugees.

Literature about the world's poor people is filled with statistics such as these. They illustrate how critical the problem of poverty really is.

We have all seen pictures of little third-world children with bloated bellies and sad eyes. The caption usually says something like this: "This little boy and millions like him will die unless you send a gift now!"

Statistics and pictures. That's about as close as many of us ever come to a meaningful confrontation with the reality of poverty. But if we are going to take the Bible seriously, we can no longer avoid this issue. We must begin to take a personal interest in the abolition of both the causes and effects of poverty.

How shall we define *poverty?* Who are the "poor"? Some have rightly discerned between *relative* poverty and *absolute* poverty. Relative poverty is determined by comparing the standards of living within a single society, such as that of the United States. Those whose standard of living is much lower than the average are considered poor even if they have all the necessities of life. According to one way of measuring, any family whose income is less than half of the national median is poor. Thus if the median family income is fourteen thousand dollars, those families making less than seven thousand are in poverty.

Absolute poverty, on the other hand, is much more serious. This refers to a situation in which one lacks even the necessities of life—where malnutrition and suffering and hopelessness are constant, and where death by starvation is a real threat.

Though there are legitimate concerns in relation to the former category, the discussion in this chapter will be limited to the problem of absolute poverty. This is sometimes referred to as the problem of world hunger, though it does extend beyond just food. It concerns those who are "without clothing and in need of daily food," those who lack "what is necessary for their body," as James 2:15, 16 puts it.

I. *God's Concern for the Poor*

The Bible has quite a bit to say about the poor, and everything it says makes it very obvious that God has a compassionate concern for them. This concern has a double focus. First, it is directed toward their state of *need;* second, it has to do with the *injustice* suffered at the hands of the rich and unscrupulous.

A. *The Poor Defended*

A famous person is reported to have said, "God must love the poor people; He made so many of them." At least part of that statement is correct: God *does* love the poor. Though the poor are of no more inherent worth than any other people, God gives special attention to them for the two reasons just mentioned.

1. *Their Greater Need*

Sometimes we refer to the poor as "the needy." Everyone has certain needs, of course; but because of unusual circumstances—for example, being a widow, an orphan, or a refugee—the needs of the poor are more acute. God is sensitive to these special needs, and He commits himself to come to their aid: "For he will deliver the needy when he cries for help, the afflicted also, and him who has no helper. He will have compassion on the poor and needy, and the lives of the needy he will save" (Ps 72:12, 13). "He raises the poor from the dust, and lifts the needy from the ash heap" (Ps 113:7).

God's ears of compassion are open: "For the Lord hears the needy, and does not despise His who are prisoners" (Ps 69:33). "'Because of the devastation of the afflicted, because of the groaning of the needy, now I will arise,' says the Lord; 'I will set him in the safety for which he longs'" (Ps 12:5).

God gave this concern concrete expression in the law of Moses when He included special provisions to meet the needs of the poor. Their needs are met in part by the law of gleaning (Lev 19:9, 10; 23:22) and the law of the fallow year (Exod 23:10, 11). The poor were allowed to give less costly offerings (Lev 5:7, 11; 12:8; 14:21, 22). Luke 2:24 says that Mary brought the lesser offering specified in Leviticus 12:8 as the sacrifice for her purification. This indicates that the very family God chose to nurture His only-begotten Son was at least relatively poor.

God is determined that the needs of the poor be met. This fact is seen in the numerous commandments to those with abundant means to give to those in need. This point will be emphasized below.

2. *Their Unjust Treatment*

Not every poor person has been treated unjustly; neither does one have to be poor to suffer injustice. However, it is a fact that poverty is often the result of unjust treatment such as robbery, discrimination, or seizure of possessions by the government. Also, the poor are usually placed in a position of helplessness where they are more vulnerable to further injustice such as price-gouging and unfair treatment from judges and other officials who take bribes from the more affluent.

This is another area of God's concern for the poor. He cares about their immediate physical needs, but he also cares when they are the victims of injustice. The psalmist declares, "I know that the Lord will maintain the cause of the afflicted, and justice for the poor" (Ps 140:12). Proverbs 22:22, 23 adds, "Do not rob the poor because he is poor, or crush the afflicted at the gate; for the Lord will plead their case, and take the life of those who rob them."

In the law of Moses, God required just treatment for the poor (Deut 24:12-15). Exodus 23:6 says, "You shall not pervert the justice due to your needy brother in his dispute." (At the same time, Exodus 23:3 warns against being partial to the poor man just because he is poor. See Lev 19:15.) Through the prophets God warned against oppressing the needy: "Thus says the Lord, 'Do justice and righteousness, and deliver the one who has been robbed from the power of his oppressor. Also do not mistreat or do violence to the stranger, the orphan, or the widow; and do not shed innocent blood in this place" (Jer 22:3).

Thus the mind of God is clear: His compassion desires that the needs of the poor be met, and His justice demands that they be treated with fairness.

B. *The Rich Condemned*

God's concern for the poor is seen not only in the positive teaching about His love and provisions for them, but also in the negative teaching that condemns the rich for their oppression and neglect of the needy. We must remember that the rich are not condemned just because they are rich, since this in itself is not wrong. They are condemned rather for the *misuse* of their wealth, especially in relation to the poor.

1. *Oppressing the Poor*

A major theme of the Old Testament prophets is the condemnation of the wicked, especially those of God's own people in Israel and Judah. One of the expressions of wickedness was their constant cheating and gouging of the poor.

The prophet Amos is usually seen as leading the way in his scathing denunciations of the oppressors. He pictures dishonest merchants, for instance, as sitting around on "holy" days, panting to open their stores in order to satisfy their greed by cheating the poor: "Hear this, you who trample the needy, to do away with the humble of the land, saying, 'When will the new moon be over, so that we may buy grain, and the sabbath, that we may open the wheat market, to make the bushel smaller and the shekel bigger, and to cheat with dishonest scales, so as to buy the helpless for money and the needy for a pair of sandals, and that we may sell the refuse of the wheat?' " (Amos 8:4-6). He condemns their ruthlessness in taking every advantage of the helpless: "Thus says the Lord, 'For three transgressions of Israel and for four I will not revoke its punishment, because they sell the righteous for money and the needy for a pair of sandals. These who pant after the very dust of the earth on the head of the helpless also turn aside the way of the humble. . . . And on garments taken as pledges they stretch out beside every altar, and in the house of their God they drink the wine of those who have been fined' " (Amos 2:6-8). Even the wives are condemned for craving luxury, thus making demands on their husbands to satisfy them even if it means robbing the poor (Amos 4:1).

From Amos come the famous words that must be heeded by any nation that hopes to endure: "Let justice roll down like waters and righteousness like an ever-flowing stream" (Amos 5:24).

But Amos is not alone in condemning the oppression of the poor. Isaiah 3:14, 15 is just as uncompromising: "The Lord enters into judgment with the elders and princes of His people: 'It is you who have devoured the vineyard; the plunder of the poor is in your houses. What do you mean by crushing My people, and grinding the face of the poor?' declares the Lord God of hosts." See also Isaiah 10:1-3: "Woe to those who enact evil statutes, and to those who constantly record unjust decisions, so as to deprive the needy of justice, and rob the poor of My people of their rights, in order that widows may be their spoil, and that they may plunder the orphans. Now what will you do in the day of punishment . . . ? And where will you leave your wealth?" Micah joins his voice with these: "Woe to those who scheme iniquity, who work out evil on their beds! When morning comes, they do it, for it is in the power of their hands. They covet fields and then seize them, and houses, and take them away. They rob a man and his house, a man and his inheritance" (Micah 2:1, 2). See also Micah 6:10-12; Jeremiah 22:13-17.

In the New Testament James 5:1-6 condemns the rich who have accumulated their wealth at the expense of the poor.

In all these words of condemnation we see not only a concern for the poor, but also a wrathful indignation against sin just because it is sin. God hates injustice, whether it is directed against the poor or the wealthy. But there is an extra dimension of depravity when the poor and needy and helpless are the victims of that injustice, and God will not allow the oppressors to go unpunished.

2. *Neglecting the Poor*

Most of us will no doubt feel quite safe from the sharp onslaughts on the prophets cited above. After all, we do not rob and cheat the poor (intentionally, at least). We are just as concerned about injustice as anyone.

But before we begin to feel too comfortable, let us note that the condemnation of the well-to-do is not limited to their *oppression* of the poor; they are also condemned for the sin of omission, for *neglecting* the poor. Proverbs 17:5 says, "He who mocks the poor reproaches his Maker." Those who are able to help the weak but do not help them are reproached by God: "Your rulers are rebels. . . . They do not defend the orphan, nor does the widow's plea come before them" (Isa 1:23). "They are fat, they are sleek, they also excel in deeds of wickedness; they do not plead the cause, the cause of the orphan, that they may prosper; and they do not defend the rights of the poor" (Jer 5:28).

Ezekiel 16:49 reveals that one of the great sins of Sodom was neglect of the poor: "Behold, this was the guilt of your sister Sodom: she and her daughters had arrogance, abundant food, and careless ease, but she did not help the poor and needy."

II. *True Religion*

God's concern for the poor is thus well established in the Bible. Now, how does God propose to meet their needs? At least in part through the generosity of His people. Those who have an abundance of this world's goods are commanded to share with the needy. James 1:27 says this is part of the essence of true religion: "This is pure and undefiled religion in the sight of our God and Father, to visit orphans and widows in their distress." We are also told to take up the cause of justice for the poor: "Learn to do good; seek justice, reprove the ruthless; defend the orphan, plead for the widow" (Isa 1:17).

A. *The Biblical Teaching*

The Law of Moses incorporated aid for the poor in its civil legislation. At harvest time, the corners and the gleanings of fields and vineyards were to be left for "the needy and the stranger" (Lev 19:9, 10). Every seventh year a field had to lie fallow. Some volunteer grain would grow from seed accidentally lost, and this could be taken by the poor "so that the needy . . . may eat" (Exod 23:10, 11). Interest was not to be charged on loans to the poor (Exod 22:25; Lev 25:36, 37). Deuteronomy 15:7-11 lays down this general rule for sharing: "If there is a poor man with you, one of your brothers, in any of your towns in your land which the Lord your God is giving you, you shall not harden your heart, nor close your hand from your poor brother; but you shall freely open your hand to him, and shall generously lend him sufficient for his need in whatever he lacks. . . . For the poor will never cease to be in the land; therefore I command you, saying, 'You shall freely open your hand to your brother, to your needy and poor in your land.' " (See Lev 25:35.)

Ezekiel 18:7 lists these marks of a righteous man (among others): he "does not oppress any one, but restores to the debtor his pledge, does not commit robbery, but gives his bread to the hungry, and covers the naked with clothing." An excellent wife, says Proverbs 31:20, "extends her hand to the poor, and she stretches out her hands to the needy." As Proverbs 29:7 says, "The righteous is concerned for the rights of the poor, the wicked does not understand such concern."

Isaiah 58:7 says that true fasting is "to divide your bread with the hungry, and bring the homeless poor into the house," and "when you see the naked, to cover him."

God promises blessings to those who help the poor: "How blessed is he who considers the helpless; the Lord will deliver him in a day of trouble" (Ps 41:1). "Happy is he who is gracious to the poor," for he honors God (Prov 14:21, 31). God will honor him in return: "He who is gracious to a poor man lends to the Lord, and He will repay him for his good deed" (Prov 19:17). "He who is generous will be blessed, for he gives some of his food to the poor" (Prov 22:9). He who neglects the poor reaps trouble, however: "He who gives to the poor will never want, but he who shuts his eyes will have many curses" (Prov 28:27).

Self-interest, of course, is not to be our motive for helping the poor. We should do it just because it is right, and because we love them in their need. That God chooses to reward us for this is just an extra bonus. (See Luke 6:35.)

The New Testament makes it clear that God expects Christians to be just as generous as the Israelites in helping the needy. Faith and love are made concrete in deeds of charity. "What use is it, my brethren, if a man says he has faith, but he has no works? Can that faith save him? If a brother or sister is without clothing and in need of daily food, and one of you says to them, 'Go in peace, be warmed and be filled,' and yet you do not give them what is necessary for their body, what use is that? Even so faith, if it has no works, is dead, being by itself" (James 2:14-17). "But whoever has the world's goods, and beholds his brother in need and closes his heart against him, how does the love of God abide in him? Little children, let us not love with word or with tongue, but in deed and truth" (I John 3:17, 18). The will of God includes our "contributing to the needs of the saints, practicing hospitality" (Rom 12:13). We should "remember the poor" (Gal 2:10) and "do good to all men" (Gal 6:10).

The saints of apostolic times set an example for benevolence that will forever challenge the church. In the earliest days those who had possessions sold them to raise cash for the needy (Acts 2:45; 4:34, 35). The widows were supplied with their daily needs (Acts 6:1-6). Paul's collection for the poor saints at Jerusalem (Rom 15:26) surely was one of the greatest fund-raising drives in church history, as Christians everywhere opened their hearts and purses to those in need (I Cor 16:1-4; II Cor 8:1—9:15).

The importance of helping the needy is seen in Jesus' depiction of the final judgment in Matthew 25:31-46. The expected evidence of saving faith (see James 2:14-26) is described as feeding the hungry, giving a drink to the thirsty, clothing the naked, showing hospitality to strangers, and visiting the sick and the prisoners. When we help the needy, says Jesus, we are showing our love for Him (Matt 25:40).

Obviously there is abundant Biblical teaching about our responsibility to help the poor. There is a need for caution, however, against overemphasizing this aspect of Scripture. In their zeal to "liberate" the poor, some have wrongly left the impression that this is the main theme of the Bible. For instance, see Ron Sider's interpretation of the exodus, the captivity, and the incarnation (*Rich Christians in an Age of Hunger;* Downers Grove: InterVarsity, 1977; pp. 60ff.). He makes such exaggerated statements as "God destroyed Israel because of mistreatment of the poor!" (page 62). This was definitely a problem in Israel, but it was only a symptom of the deeper problem of rebellion against the true God. Spiritual poverty, spiritual blindness, and spiritual captivity are infinitely more serious than their physical counterparts; these spiritual problems are the main target of the incarnation (Luke 4:17-19).

B. *The Church's Responsibility*

In view of this Biblical teaching, how can Christians today carry out their responsibilities toward the poor?

1. *Correcting Injustice*

One thing that must be remembered is that the church's main task is evangelism, while it is the God-ordained role of government to preserve justice. (See Jack Cottrell, *Tough Questions—Biblical Answers,* vol. II, to be published by College Press in 1986.) "Social justice" is not the church's main agenda, though this statement is contrary to a major trend in theology today.

The church can fulfill a prophetic role today by acting as the conscience of the state. That is, Christians and the church should speak out against injustice and encourage government to perform its duty in this regard. This does not, however, give individuals or groups the right to break the law in protest or as an attention-getting device. Nor does it give anyone the right, in the name of Christianity or otherwise, to promote the violent overthrow of any government. One of the saddest perversions of Christian concern today is the collaboration of many so-called Christian groups with Marxist revolutionaries in third-world areas. There appears to be a willingness to sacrifice spiritual values and personal freedoms on the altar of "economic equality." What a triumph for materialism!

It is true that much injustice exists, and it is true that the church must be concerned about it. But the picture is complicated by sharp disagreement as to the exact nature of this injustice. Some think that any form of economic inequality is unjust; thus they seek to influence government toward socialism or toward more taxation and redistribution of wealth via welfare and foreign aid. But we have already seen that inequality per se (which may include *relative* poverty) is not unjust. In fact, some feel that taxation for this purpose is itself unjust, as is socialism, since it violates the principle of work as the means of ownership.

Examples of poverty-causing injustice on which most would agree are the exploitation of migrant workers by unscrupulous overseers, discrimination (racist or otherwise) that deprives anyone of work opportunities, and judicial systems weighted against the poor. Christians can encourage governments to correct such wrongs as these while they seek better understanding and more unanimity on the controversial issues.

2. *Feeding the Hungry*

Though the church's main task is evangelism, it does have a secondary responsibility of feeding the hungry and helping the poor. A portion of every local congregation's budget should be designated for benevolence, as distinct from missions. There should also be a readiness on the part of all members to meet emergency needs as the occasion arises.

Though no one should be turned down in a real emergency, the church's principal obligation in the area of benevolence is toward those of the "household of the faith" (Gal 6:10), that is, fellow Christians. James 2:15, I John 3:17, and Matthew 25:40 speak of feeding *brothers and sisters* who are hungry. These are brothers and sisters in a spiritual sense, and not everyone is included. (See Matt 12:50.)

The early church's considerable benevolent activity seems to have been mainly for the poor *saints* (Rom 15:26). It was *those who believed* who had all things in common (Acts 2:44). We should not forget, though, that this responsibility extended to brethren everywhere; Paul's collection for the poor saints in Jerusalem was international in scope. (See I Cor 16:1; II Cor 8:1-3.)

In "good Samaritan" emergencies one does not ask the religious status of the person in need. Such cases provide opportunities to "do good to all men," but they do not diminish our greater responsibility to "those who are of the household of faith" (Gal 6:10). (On the question of non-responsibility toward the unbelieving poor, see Isa 9:17; Prov 10:3.)

An unbeliever's main need is spiritual, and the church's primary responsibility toward him is evangelism. This is not callousness; it is simply a realistic recognition of proper priorities.

This does not rule out all help for the unbelieving poor. Indeed, there may be occasions where feeding the hungry is a necessary prerequisite to preaching the gospel, and there may be times when it opens the door to evangelism. We refer to this as *evangelistic benevolence.* This is an area that ought to be expanded mightily, since it enables the church to perform its main task while showing compassion on the materially needy at the same time. An agency that attempts to combine these two purposes in this way is IDES (International Disaster Emergency Service), 106 W. Jefferson, Box 60, Kempton, IN 46049.

How can individual Christians become more involved in the task of feeding the hungry? First, they can encourage the church to strengthen its benevolent program, and they can give toward it (Eph 4:28; I Tim 6:18; I Cor 16:2; Acts 20:35). Second, they can (if they wish) become involved in governmental or independent relief programs, such as Food First, Food for the Hungry, Bread for the World, or World Vision. This activity must not become a substitute for working through the local church, however. Third, they can commit themselves to develop a less wasteful, more moderate life-style. This subject will be discussed further in the next chapter.

13

ECOLOGY

If you have ever followed a vehicle that belched billows of blue smoke, if you have ever gagged at the stench of a polluted stream, if you have ever wheezed your way through smog, if you have ever waited in a long line to buy overpriced gasoline, if you have ever seen a seabird disabled by an oil slick—then you know what this chapter is all about. It deals with the ecological crisis, also called the environmental crisis.

The latter part of this book has been dealing with certain ethical problems relating to stewardship, especially of time and money. In this final chapter we are still dealing with stewardship, but the scope has broadened considerably. The issue here is stewardship of the *earth.* What responsibility do we as human beings have for the proper use and preservation of the earth and its resources?

The answer to this question comes from the one who made the heavens and the earth in the first place. In the Bible He gives us the basic core of our "environmental ethic." Thus the Bible is like a manufacturer's handbook, providing instructions on how to use and maintain the product. Here we will attempt to summarize these instructions and suggest ways to implement them.

I. *The Crisis*

Exactly what is meant by the term *environmental crisis?* It has at least two aspects. First, it refers to man's pollution of the environment by dumping unnatural kinds or amounts of wastes into it. The air is polluted with engine exhausts, industrial emissions, excessive noise, wastes from burning coal, radiation, and cigarette smoke. Water is polluted by raw sewage, detergents, pesticides, chemical wastes, industrial offal, oil spills, and garbage of all kinds. Such pollution poses both short- and long-range dangers to mankind as well as to wildlife.

The other aspect of the crisis is the dwindling supply of non-renewable natural resources such as metals and fossil fuels. The potential exhaustion of fossil fuel (coal, oil, and gas) leads us to talk about the energy crisis. We could also include the problem of endangered species here, since animals are a kind of natural resource.

It is customary to use the word *crisis* to refer to this problem. Just how serious is it? Is it truly a crisis? There are extreme answers to these questions. Some observers are known as "doomsayers"; they say the crisis is extremely serious and that the world will not last long unless radical steps are taken *now.* In the early 1970's a study called *The Limits of Growth* projected that around A.D. 2020 society will begin to collapse because of pollution and depleted resources. We are warned that continuing pollution will ultimately lead to the death of the oceans, which will then cause the rest of the earth to die. Thus we are committing terracide.

At the other extreme are those who declare that the doomsayers are just "crying wolf" and that we really have nothing to worry about. The problem is not that serious. Dr. John McKetta, a chemical engineer and past chairman of the National Air Quality Management Committee, says the ecological crisis is mostly myth. "From what we read and hear it would seem we are on the edge of impending doom. A scientific evaluation of the evidence does not support this conclusion," he says. Indeed, a 1982 Nairobi meeting of scientists and environmentalists has pronounced the oceans to be in very good shape and hardly affected at all by pollution.

What is the answer? It probably lies somewhere between extreme pessimism and extreme optimism. We may not be on the edge of doom, but the problem is still quite serious, no doubt a lot more serious than most people realize. Perhaps it is premature to project the extinction of the human race, but pollution surely endangers the health of many of us and even the lives of some. And there is no questioning the fact that we *are* depleting the world's supply of natural resources, particularly its coal and oil. We may not be able to predict how long they will last, but the resources *are* finite. Even if we have enough for our generation, we cannot adopt the philosophy, "Let us eat and drink, for tomorrow we die" (I Cor 15:32). It is a question of justice: it is unjust for us to waste resources that will be needed by future generations.

(We will not include the question of endangered species in the crisis category. All species have some value, and the loss of any of them is sad to those who witness it. However, the extinction of some species is not a threatening evil. The fossil evidence suggests that perhaps as many as a hundred million species disappeared over the millennia. This is more of an emotional than a practical problem.)

It is appropriate, then, to speak of a *crisis.* It is serious enough that every one of us must seek to understand it and join in the effort to resolve it.

II. *The Cause*

When we inquire into the cause of the ecological crisis, the first two suggestions to be encountered are runaway technology and over-population. We may grant that these are contributing factors, but for the real cause we must probe more deeply into the heart of man himself. The crisis is the result of certain attitudes and values that have dominated Western thinking in particular.

At this point we will mention a theory that will surprise and perhaps even anger most Christians. It is the thesis introduced by Lynn White, Jr., in an article entitled "The Historical Roots of Our Ecologic Crisis" (*Science;* March 10, 1967; pp. 1203-1207). White agrees that the basic cause of the crisis is a specific set of ideas and values, and he says those ideas are found *in the Bible.* Biblical teaching, especially the Judeo-Christian doctrine of creation, has caused the ecological crisis!

How could this be? Well, says White, before Christianity permeated Western thinking, "pagans" everywhere looked upon nature as more or less sacred and filled with spirits (animism). The supposed spirits in a real sense protected nature from man. But Biblical religion changed all that. According to Genesis, God made the natural universe; but then He made man as something separate from nature. Nature was made only to serve man, and man was made to rule over nature.

This set the stage for man's exploitation of his environment. Says White, "Christianity . . . insisted that it is God's will that man exploit nature for his proper ends." When Christianity destroyed pagan animism, "the old inhibitions to the exploitation of nature crumbled." Man considered himself "superior to nature, contemptuous of it, willing to use it" for his "slightest whim." Thus "Christianity bears a huge burden of guilt," and the crisis will only get worse until we reject this "orthodox Christian arrogance toward nature."

What shall we say to this rather startling accusation? Any Christian who even halfway knows his Bible will see immediately that White has greatly misunderstood the implications of Genesis 1 and is woefully ignorant of the total Biblical teaching about man and nature. As George Alder says in his excellent series on "Our Fragile Earth" in *The Lookout* (January 11, 18, 25, 1981), "The critics have not read the Bible carefully."

The Biblical ethic does not sanction the exploitation of nature. The crisis has been caused not by those who understand and follow the Bible, but by those who misinterpret it or ignore it. An editorial in *Christianity Today* (April 23, 1971; p. 26) sums it up: "The values system that is at the root of our environmental troubles does not come from the Judeo-Christian tradition. . . . The fault lies not with revealed religion but with those who insist on a life style that is at odds with it." This would be a life-style characterized by greed, selfishness, materialism, autonomy, and consumeritis—all of which are contrary to Biblical teaching, not justified by it as White and others allege.

III. *The Cure*

The Biblical doctrine of nature, rather than the cause of the environmental crisis, is the cure for it. Unfortunately, what the Bible says on this subject is not widely recognized, not even among Christians. We should want to formulate and follow the Scriptural teaching about nature, even if there were no crisis to deal with. That there *is* a crisis makes this even more imperative.

A. *The Fact of Creation*

The primary element in the Biblical ethic is indeed the fact of creation. White was right to identify this as the crucial doctrine, though he was wrong in his interpretation of it. The fact that the natural universe is a creation of God is the foundation of the only proper attitude toward it, namely, *respect.* As Francis Schaeffer says in his book, *Pollution and the Death of Man* (Downers Grove: Inter-Varsity, 1970), "We treat it with respect because God made it" (p. 76).

We dare not approach nature with arrogance, contempt, or indifference, contrary to White's characterization of the Christian view. It is the good creation of the good God (Gen 1:31); he himself cares about its smallest details (Matt 10:29). We respect it because God respects it.

On the other hand, just because it is *created,* we approach nature *only* with respect and not with reverence. We do not personify or deify it, or invest it with any untouchable sacredness. Among many environmentalists there is an attitude toward nature that approaches pantheism; they have made all of nature into a sacred cow. A *Christianity Today* editorial (April 10, 1970; p. 33) calls this "ecologism" and says it is no more than "old-fashioned paganism."

Let us be careful that we do not make nature an end in itself. After all, God created it for His own glory and for the good of mankind.

B. *Stewardship of the Earth*

The facts are that the earth *was* created to serve man, and man *is* above or over or superior to all the rest of the natural universe. These are clear Biblical teachings; they are not scandalous, nor are they a license for exploitation. Man, being created in the image of God, was appointed to subdue the earth and have dominion over it (Gen 1:27, 28). There can never be equality between man and nature (despite the "Brother Earth" idea).

But—and this is a crucial point—neither can man ever have *absolute* authority or "limitless rule" over creation, to use another of White's parodies of Christianity. Man has dominion over the earth, but not sovereignty. God is still the Creator, and He alone is sovereign over His creation—man and nature alike. "The earth is the Lord's, and all it contains, the world, and those who dwell in it" (Ps 24:1).

Thus man does not own the earth, nor is he free to do whatever he chooses with it. Man is only a *steward.* He *tends* the earth (cultivates and keeps it—Gen 2:15), for his own benefit to be sure, but also for the glory of God. We should treat it with care and respect not just for pragmatic reasons (so we won't destroy ourselves) but because we as stewards will have to answer to the owner some day.

In view of our responsibilities as stewards of the earth we must recognize that it *is* wrong to pollute our environment, and not just for selfish reasons. Pollution is vandalism of God's property. It is just as wrong in principle to toss a wrapper or can out a car window as to dump chemicals in a stream.

We must also see that it is wrong to waste the resources placed in our care. They are meant to be used, of course; that is why God included a stock of ores and coal and oil in the earth. But they were not meant to be abused and wasted by planned obsolescence and gluttonous consumption.

C. *The Right Priorities*

George Alder has rightly noted, "Even though we present an adequate defense, so that the Bible is not judged the culprit for all these evils, we Christians are not off the hook. It is one thing for us to defend the Biblical view and quite another to demonstrate conformity to that view."

Quite so! Stewardship of the earth is not an easy task, and we all seem to be falling woefully short. How can we change this? The key lies in the final element in the Bible's environmental ethic, namely, a proper ordering of values. Only when we get our priorities straight will the environmental crisis be under control.

The Biblical ethic demands that *material* concerns be subordinated to *spiritual* ones. We must seek heavenly treasures, not earthly ones (Matt 6:19, 20). "Set your mind on the things above, not on the things that are on earth" (Col 3:2). "Do not love the world, nor the things in the world" (I John 2:15). Life does not consist of our possessions (Luke 12:15).

This is a strong indictment of our materialistic values: our obsession with the gross national product and our standard of living; our love of affluence, luxuries, and baubles; our pursuit of unlimited economic growth; our indulgence in status symbols and conspicuous consumption. Can we give these up? *We must!*—if we hope to fulfill our stewardship.

The Biblical ethic also demands that we take account of the needs of others, as we saw in the last chapter. In this case we must remember the needs of future generations; we must not steal from them just to satisfy our craving for material luxuries (Exod 20:15).

What are some specific ways in which we can practice our stewardship and conquer our materialism? For one thing, we can take a real interest in environmental problems and try to become informed about them. Many issues are extremely complex. An example of this is nuclear energy, which presents a kind of dilemma: it offers a solution to the problem of disappearing resources, but seems to aggravate the problem of pollution. (What shall we do with the radioactive wastes?)

For another thing, we can support conservation organizations and programs. One concrete way to do this is to become committed to recycling, even if it costs a little more in time and effort. Recycle paper; recycle cans. Don't buy throw-away bottles.

Finally, and perhaps most significantly, we can work toward a simpler life-style. This will enable us not only to conserve energy and resources, but also to have more to share with those who are in need.

We are talking about godly moderation and careful consumption. The fact that we have the money to spend does not justify our buying every little trinket or big luxury item that catches our eye. We should buy fewer things and keep them longer. We should practice joint ownership of little-used items such as ladders and certain tools. Small things count: use both sides of writing paper; ride the bus; eat the leftovers; turn off the shower while soaping up; turn out the lights! And do these things not just to save money, but to save the earth!

For even more radical suggestions (sometimes too radical), see books such as *Living More Simply* (Downers Grove: InterVarsity, 1980) and *Lifestyle in the Eighties* (Philadelphia: Westminster, 1982), both edited by Ron Sider. The latter includes this thoughtful resolution: "We resolve to renounce waste and oppose extravagance in personal living, clothing and housing, travel and church buildings. We also accept the distinction between necessities and luxuries, creative hobbies and empty status symbols, modesty and vanity, occasional celebrations and normal routine, and between the service of God and slavery to fashion" (p. 16).

We recognize, of course, that the ultimate solution to the environmental crisis will be the new heavens and new earth (II Peter 3:10-13), when "the creation itself also will be set free from its slavery to corruption" (Rom 8:21). But in the meantime, let us do our best to glorify God through our conscientious care for the old earth!